TERRAIN
MODELLING

OSPREY MASTERCLASS

TERRAIN
MODELLING

Richard Windrow

Dedication
To my brother Martin, who said I should do it.
To my wife Avril, who said I could do it, if I tried.
And to my old friend Charles Davis, who lent me
the camera and enabled me to do it.

© 2001 Osprey Publishing Limited

First published in 2001
by Osprey Publishing,
Elms Court, Chapel Way,
Botley, Oxford OX2 9LP, UK

Editor: Martin Windrow
Design: Frank Ainscough/Compendium
Printed in China through World Print Ltd.
01 02 03 04 05   10 9 8 7 6 5 4 3 2 1

FOR A CATALOGUE OF ALL TITLES
PUBLISHED BY OSPREY MILITARY
AND AVIATION PLEASE WRITE TO:
The Marketing Manager, Osprey Publishing Ltd,
PO Box 140, Wellingborough,
Northants NN8 4ZA, United Kingdom
E-mail: info@OspreyDirect.co.uk

The Marketing Manager, Osprey Direct USA,
PO Box 130, Sterling Heights,
MI 48311-0130, United States of America
E-mail: info@OspreyDirectUSA.com

www.ospreypublishing.com

A CIP catalogue record of this book
is available from the British Library

ISBN 1 84176 062 5

CONTENTS

INTRODUCTION

Like me, I am sure you have seen many an excellent model - whether 'kit-bashed' or 'scratch-built' - spoiled by being placed in a setting that does it little or no justice. How often have we seen a beautifully painted mounted figure of a Napoleonic hussar, placed on a lifeless stretch of green 'lawn' with no variation in colour or length? Or 45 tons of Panther tank parked on turf on which it has not made a single track mark - how did it get there? Was it lowered by a crane? By this lack of imagination and failure to go the last mile the creator of what may be a prize-standard model sabotages the whole aim of his many hours of effort - to create an accurate impression in miniature of a tank on the battlefield. It is heartbreaking to see a brilliantly made and painted model set in an embarassingly unsuccessful attempt to reproduce miniature terrain, so that the contrast instantly destroys any impression of realism.

These mistakes are seldom committed because the modeller is too lazy, or doesn't care how the finished scene will look. All modellers want the end result of their work to show to the best advantage. I believe that the primary reason they make these mistakes is because while many modellers have excellent reference sources for figures or vehicles, when it comes to the setting they probably have no references at all, and don't think about that problem until it is too late. Couldn't the chap who made the Napoleonic hussar have found a picture of an 18th century country lane, rather than placing his superb figure on an uninspiring strip of astroturf? None of us would attempt to build the model without some pictorial reference, so why should we have to make the rest of the diorama from our imaginations? It's much easier to look at pictures; modify them to suit your own particular purpose, by all means, but give yourself a sound basis on which to work.

ABOUT THIS BOOK

The purpose of this book is to try to help any of you who have difficulty in reproducing the great outdoors in your dioramas. The method I have adopted is to model, and take step-by-step photos of, a number of areas of different kinds of terrain - in most cases, as 6in x 8in vignettes - to illustrate the way I work. This size suits the popular scale of 1/35th, and saved me from the impossible pressure of making a couple of dozen fullsize dioramas specifically for the book. At the same time I have included photos of some already finished dioramas; and also a few outdoor shots, which I hope will inspire you to gather your own useful references for future projects.

Obviously, in a book of this size and with the time available, I have not been able to show an example of every type of terrain that you might possibly wish to model, but I hope I have been able to cover many of the main subjects. The methods used are, I believe, fairly simple and don't call for any painfully expensive tools or materials. Virtually all the materials I've used here are readily available in the UK, and I have included an Appendix at the end of the book which lists where I obtained the various brands and products.

The chapters are organised in a roughly logical sequence; but the method of working through a series of vignettes has prevented me from keeping each aspect of terrain rigidly in its own section. In particular, note that water effects are covered in a number of chapters apart from the specific descriptions in Chapter 8 - e.g. in Chapter 2, where I incorporated a

rushing torrent among the rock effects; in Chapter 7, where the jungle shrouds a swamp or sluggish stream; and in Chapter 9, where I cover beach scenes. In the same way, trees receive detailed attention to Chapters 5 and 7 as well as Chapter 4.

In describing the more basic processes I have tried not to repeat myself too often, so the chapters are probably best read in sequence; if I seem to rush through the explanation of some particular step, check back - it is probably covered more fully in an earlier chapter.

In my long and sometimes frustrating years of modelling I have come across many tips and ideas for creating realistic terrain for my dioramas, and I make no claim for originality in what follows. Some of the effects shown here are indeed of my own invention; many are not, so if you come across your brainchild in these pages, my apologies, but I'm sure you would not begrudge my passing it on to a wider audience.

I should like to add a couple of final points. The first concerns the matter of colour. Those members of the modelling fraternity who build, say, tanks, attempt to match the colour schemes as accurately as possible to contemporary references, colour chips or colour photographs. Articles in modelling magazines often give you the exact percentage of the different colours to mix to obtain the finished shade. When I set out to build a diorama I'm afraid I can't do this - because Mother Nature doesn't either. I look at my references for a particular scene, and then I mix colours and apply them to the groundwork until it satisfies my eye. It is a question of trial and error, but you will find that this is not nearly as difficult as it may sound; you will know when the thing looks right, and that is when to stop.

The second point concerns the type and period of modelling subjects you choose. While my own interests lie in the wars of the 20th century, modelled in 1/35th scale, the basic methods and materials I show here can be used - with a few minor modifications - for creating miniature settings for virtually any subject, military or civilian, at any period of history, and in all popular scales.

ACKNOWLEDGEMENTS

No book is the work of the author alone, and this one is no exception. I am most grateful for the assistance of a number of people, but first and foremost must be my brother Martin who, in his role as 'Attila the Editor', encouraged me into writing this book and then translated it into a readable version of the Queen's English. My wife Avril showed an almost inhuman patience, as I used all our spare evenings and weekends to model, photograph and write - I promise we'll go out next year. Others who have been most helpful include Charles Davis (who whittled more sticks for palisades than you can imagine), Barry Bowen, Lyn Sangster of Historex Agents, Tim Hawkins, Gerry Embleton, Roy Dixon, Bob Wyatt of Scale Link, and Dominique Breffort of *Figurines* magazine. Thanks also to Adrian of Seymour Harrison Photographers, and John at Andrew Colour Laboratories, who both answered my idiotic questions on photography with unfailing cheerfulness.

Richard Windrow
Folkestone, Kent
January 2001

CHAPTER 1
PREPARATION, MATERIALS & TECHNIQUES

REFERENCES

You cannot build a convincing piece of model terrain from memory or imagination. As with the building of any model, the first thing you need is good reference, both historical and geographical. To take an obvious example, a European modeller who decides to build a diorama of the landings on Iwo Jima is certainly going to need pictorial reference if he hopes for a convincing finish (incidentally, the sand was black).

Put together a collection of pictures of natural surroundings, taken in different types of terrain, at different seasons and in different weathers. For World War II and postwar subjects colour photos from old issues of magazines such as *The National Geographic* are immensely useful and well worth collecting, as are black and white shots from *Life* and *Picture Post*; back numbers of all these can be picked up quite cheaply at second hand bookshops and

BELOW RIGHT Unsurfaced tracks nearly always show a strip of scuffed grass between the wheel tracks - throughout history up to the 19th century (and often thereafter) most roads used by armies have been unsurfaced ones like this.

BELOW The edge of a field in early autumn. The grass doesn't just 'stop' when it reaches the hedge; a fringe of long, yellowish wisps grows out of still-green shorter grass and weeds, passing out of sight under the bushes or hedge. (Thanks to Gerry Embleton for taking all the 'real terrain' photos in this book.)

boot fairs. Well illustrated travel and natural history books showing most corners of the earth can be found easily in public libraries. Films and videos can also be a good source of reference; you'll be surprised at how much background detail you can see if you ignore the main action.

If you have friends living in Britain or abroad in countryside which differs from your own region, ask them to take photos for you of their part of the world; in this way you can build up a good reference library for future use. I recently picked up a small pack of colour post-cards taken in jungle and rainforest, which gave me some excellent reference on tropical trees and jungle floor growth. Such photos don't have to be limited to natural surroundings, of course; get hold of pictures of airfields, military ranges, castle moats, derelict farm buildings, factories, anything you can think of - you will be sure to find a use for it one day.

Old paintings reproduced in books and catalogues can be a great help when modelling periods of history that pre-date the camera. The basics of terrain may not change over the centuries, but the look of the countryside certainly does - roads and lanes, bridges, walls, hedges and other field boundaries, and patterns of cultivation are all characteristic of their regions and periods. It would be a shame to set your model 15th century knights against a post-18th century hedge.

An obvious point is that even when you are going about your normal daily round you should keep your eyes open. You may assume that you know what 'landscape' looks like; but most of us live in towns these days, and we can't summon up automatically an accurate mental picture of the details of the countryside which we need if we are to make convincing model settings. No opportunity to 'scout locations' for your modelling should be missed. The colour and texture of different tree trunks, the variety of coloured grasses and weeds in a single meadow, the appearance of a hedge covered in frost - notice them all.

Look at the grass alongside most roads and tracks: the first few inches are nearly always a dead yellow-tan colour, which slowly grades into shades of green as it gets further from the edge. Under hedges you'll find that the grass is long and wispy where it hasn't been cut, and is filled with leaf litter. On country tracks a central strip is often untrodden and covered with scruffy grass. On stony paths the larger stones will tend to be up the centre strip and along either side, leaving the smaller gravel in the two flanking tracks ground down by wheeled traffic or pedestrians. Most military movement in any period before the 20th century took place on such unsurfaced roads.

A second good reason to keep your eyes open when you are out and about on foot is, of course, to spot useful-shaped twigs, etc., to turn into trees. It might raise a few eyebrows when your friends see you diving into the gutter every now and then, but it's worth it. If you are lucky enough to live near the coast, try to pick up small pieces of bleached driftwood; these are excellent for modelling deadfalls and branches in your forest scenes. Trying to reproduce that wonderful silvery colour of old, dead wood can be tricky, so why not use the real thing? (The fallen tree trunk in the 'Icy Pond' vignette on page 121 is a piece of sea-polished driftwood.)

TOOLS

The tools which I use to create groundwork are simple, inexpensive and easily obtainable. You need a jug for water, plastic mixing bowls for plaster or Celluclay, and cheap throwaway brushes - for spreading plaster and Celluclay and for colouring the results. It's not worth getting decent ones clogged with paste and plaster. Spatulas and a fairly flexible oil painter's palette knife are also useful for applying and shaping the groundwork, and most art and craft shops will have these in stock. If you're on good terms with your friendly neighbourhood dentist then have a word with him and see if he has any old dental tools to spare; these are very handy for some of the smaller tasks and more delicate shaping you may wish to do. It is always a good idea to have at least two modelling knives to hand; I personally use the brass Swan Moreton type with Nos.10, 10A, 11 & 26 blades. You won't use these as much as you would when building a model kit, but they are a useful addition to your toolkit nonetheless.

A spray bottle of some kind to 'mist' water and/or thinned out PVA glue is handy; but if you use it for glue give it a good wash out with warm water as soon as you finish, or you'll find the nozzle is completely clogged the next time you reach for it. Woodland Scenics sell a spray bottle for use with their 'Scenic Cement' (see Materials, below). This makes the coverage of

large areas much easier than dabbing away with a paint brush.

While on the subject of spraying, I came across a very useful piece of kit in an arts and crafts shop some while ago: a rechargeable aerosol spray. You just unscrew the top, fill with water or Scenic Cement and replace the cap, then pump up the pressure with the pump provided. It has a very small nozzle and this enables you to just 'mist' the liquid over your scene, rather than blasting a jet of water across it. I find this particularly useful if I have a large area of plaster to paint, such as a rock face. Before applying the paint, mist water to which you've added a small drop of washing up liquid over the whole piece, and you'll find that your colours will key into the plaster much better than if painted onto a dry surface.

BELOW The real thing. Get off the beaten track and use your eyes - these mossy rocks and sinister 'Arthur Rackham' roots offer dramatic settings for a single figure or a small group creeping through the woods in any historical period.

RIGHT Old paintings and prints reveal terrain details which can make all the difference. This is the Waterloo road in 1815 - note the wide verge of churned-up earth each side of the paved carriageway, typical of highroads throughout Europe in the 17th to 19th centuries (see pages 107-109).

A flour shaker is ideal for spreading fine 'ground cover', snow and static grass. It lets you sift on a nice even coating and prevents lumps and clumps from forming. I picked one up in Boots the chemists for about £1.50. I use a pestle and mortar, bought in a kitchen supply shop, for grinding up dried leaves and herbs when I need 'scatter' to go under a hedge or leaf litter on a forest floor. This is much quicker than crushing it between your fingers, and you can get the pieces much finer.

Another useful gadget I picked up in a kitchen supply shop is called a cakemaker's turntable over here, but I believe in the States they are referred to as 'Lazy Susans'. Intended to be used when icing cakes, they make ideal bases on which to stand a model while you're adding stuff. You can keep your hands off the groundwork and turn the model to any angle you like without knocking lumps off or leaving fingerprints in the fresh plaster.

Finally, I always keep an old hair-drier to hand. It is very useful sometimes for 'hurrying things along', and for creating ripples in 'water'. I picked one up in a junk shop – I wouldn't dare liberate the other one in the house.

MATERIALS & TECHNIQUES

The materials you use to create your scene can be as cheap or expensive as you care to make them. Shep Paine, the 'grand master' of American diorama modellers, was once asked what he used to achieve such realistic dirt effects; he replied, 'dirt'. Where you can, use the real thing. The bamboo stems in the 'Cave-Busters' diorama on page 81 are actual stems from a miniature bamboo in my garden, with paper leaves added. Good effects can be achieved with all kinds of twigs, roots, dried plants, etc., and it is always worth checking the dried flower stock at your local florist's shop. At the other end of the scale, you can buy very detailed photo-etched brass foliage and complete tree kits, but these will naturally cost you rather more.

The accompanying photos show a variety of the materials that I use, including grass and gravel matting, static grass, ground cover, polyfibre, plaster of Paris, Celluclay, plaster bandage, white PVA glue, and various other items. These come from hobby companies, model shops, florists' and doll's house suppliers, and are all fairly easy to obtain. Rather than repeating the same basic advice over and again as I describe the different vignettes in subsequent chapters, brief explanations of the use of these materials follow here. (**For sources of all products mentioned in this chapter, see the Appendix on page 128**).

Glues You will obviously need different glues from time to time when building your dioramas. Mostly it will be the good old white PVA as found in every DIY shop in the land, and my favourites are Loctite's Wood Bond Rapid or Evo-Stik Extra Fast Wood Adhesive. On occasion you'll want a glue that can be sprayed onto the groundwork; you can, of course, just let down your PVA with water, but I tend to use Woodland Scenics' Scenic Cement. This is, almost certainly, simply a thinned-out PVA; but it gives me just the right consistency every time, and rather than fiddling about mixing my own I can just pour this into a spray container and I'm in business, with the excess going back into the bottle. Another good point is that it dries to a matt finish, so you don't get the light picking up sparkly reflections among your bushes.

In a later chapter I describe the use of another specialist adhesive marketed by Woodland Scenics, called Hob-e-Tac, so I won't repeat myself here.

Grass Matting This can be bought from most model railway suppliers, model shops and several craft companies; the particular matting illustrated is from Gaugemaster. It is useful to use as an underlay when you have fairly large areas of flat grass to put down, such as on an airfield. You can vary the colour and texture of this by adding patches of static grass to it, or dry-brushing a contrasting shade lightly over it in a random fashion. Another useful trick is to wet an area of the matting - say in the shape of a path, or a circular patch for a gun emplacement. Leave it to soak in for a while and then, using a spatula of some kind, scrape over the damp surface; the grass will peel off, leaving you with a clear area to work with.

Similarly, **Gravel Matting** is usually used to represent ballast under the tracks on a model railway layout, but it can also be used for any gravelled area you want - paths, parking areas for trucks, and so on. Like the grass matting it is glued to a tough paper backing; it can be cut with ordinary scissors to shape it and is flexible enough to follow the contours of your groundwork.

Ground Cover I often use 'ground covers' from Woodland Scenics in the USA, which are made from ground-up latex rubber. These are available in a wide range of colours and textures, enabling you build up from very light cover representing grass to very coarse cover for weeds. I'm not quite so keen on using the extra coarse for bushes or shrubs, since I prefer to make these up from wire, plaster and poly-fibre; but, this said, our friends at

Woodland Scenics do produce an amazing range of excellent materials. They stick very easily with PVA glue, and are quite economical as well. Just place your diorama on a sheet of newspaper and scatter your ground cover on. When the glue has dried, carefully tip the model, or blow gently across it; you can shake the surplus off the paper and keep it for another day.

Ground cover is also useful for making foliage for your trees. I usually use photo-mount sprayed onto the frame of the tree, stick on poly-fibre, spray once again, and then scatter some of the finer flocks onto the fibre. This is the lazy man's way, of course; for trees which look like the real thing, see Chapter 4.

Static Grass This is also available in a range of colours, from bright spring shades to dead winter tones. It is made from nylon flock and is best applied with a shaker, onto areas of your model over which you have previously sprayed an adhesive. If you drift it on from your hand or a spatula it tends to clump. I should warn

ABOVE This turntable came from a kitchen supply shop. It is ideal for rotating your model, enabling you to work on any aspect of it without getting your fingers in wet groundwork.

BELOW Virtually all the tools I use for my dioramas. On the left is the 'Arty's' refillable aerosol mentioned in the text (see also Appendix on page 128). The tools in the centre all came from the 4D Model Shop and are ideal for spreading and shaping small areas of ground-work. On the right are spatulas and an artist's palette knife from my local art shop. The clear jar with the perforated disc in front is for scattering large areas of static grass or some of the finer ground covers. Glass mixing rods are great for stirring up Celluclay or plaster as they wipe clean so easily.

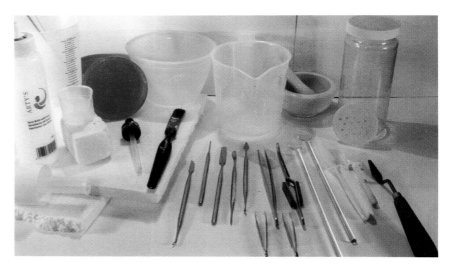

Very basic work with grass mat:
(1) damping an area to be 'shaved' for a track;
(2) the 'grass' is scraped off, leaving the paper backing;
(3) a neat gravel path is added from Talus ground cover stuck down with PVA.

RIGHT Rubberised horsehair, used for making a low tangle of bushes.

RIGHT Plaster bandage, used over rough formers as the basis for a frozen riverbank scene.

you, though, that however you apply it, it drifts everywhere; so make sure you apply your glue to the exact part of your model that you want to grass over, otherwise you'll find you've got it growing on your buildings, figures, tanks and anything else in sight. As soon as you have applied the grass, blow gently across the model from one side; this will cause the little fibres to stand up, creating a very realistic effect. You can obtain a nice appearance of varied grasses in one plot by mixing the various colours, and by dry-brushing once it has dried.

Another material available is **Field Grass**. This is finer and longer than static grass, and I use it anywhere that tall reeds or grasses are needed. It is available in a shade of green or a light tan, but you can colour it with acrylic paint if you want different finishes.

Poly-fibre This is a very fine nylon-like wadding which, when teased out, is ideal for the basis of tree foliage, bushes, etc., and can also be used for ground cover. Stretch it out far enough and you can use it for vines and creepers on your hillside or jungle floor, or as a base cover on the framework of a hedge. You can add any type of flock or leaf scatter to it with PVA glue to create different kinds of foliage.

Rubberised Horsehair This material has a hundred-and-one uses, but you will probably bless it for enabling you to create (at last) realistic brambles, tangled undergrowth and hedges. It is available in blocks or in hedge-like strips, and can be secured to the groundwork with PVA. It is covered with small, uneven blobs of what I assume to be dried adhesive - this merely adds to the appearance of leaves growing. Tangled ground cover is one of the hardest types of growth to model convincingly; it is seldom, if ever, just one layer of a single growth. Look at bushes and hedges: some grow vertically, some at an angle and some horizontally. They grow into each other and mingle with the growth under them. To make realistic tangled undergrowth you must add it to your diorama in layers, starting with the grass or weeds and working your way up to the coarsest or tallest growth - in other words, do it the way nature does it.

One more thing: as far as I'm concerned, lichen is only good for making camel thorn bushes in a desert scene or a prickly growth in a jungle setting. A strip of green lichen for a hedge just doesn't do the job.

Celluclay I must admit to a great liking for working with Celluclay. Originally only available from the USA, but now to be found in many UK outlets, Celluclay is a packet of instant *papier maché* which you mix with water, as you would plaster, but unlike plaster it does not set to such a smooth finish. Unless you are modelling ice or still water you want a textured finish to your groundwork, and Celluclay can be controlled to give you as 'lumpy' a finish as you want. Another bonus with this product is that, unlike plaster, if you mix up too much for the job in hand you can just leave it in the bowl; the addition of water will bring it back to a workable texture, after any interval up to about a week. If you can't find a stockist of Celluclay near you, a good alternative is Claycrete, made by the American Art Clay Co. of Indianapolis, USA. This is another instant *papier maché* and is also available in arts and crafts shops in Britain.

Plaster Both plaster and plaster bandage, which both set after the addition of water, will almost certainly be necessary for your dioramas. While Celluclay is excellent for the basic soil areas of the model, for your rocks and cliffs you need something tougher which can be shaped, sanded and painted. I prefer the plaster bandage as it sets much quicker than thick layers of powdered plaster. This can be found in most good chemists' shops, and this is usually a cheaper way to buy it than in brand-named packs in model shops.

Dampen the bandage in a bowl of water and drape it over the shape of your slope or hillside; it will naturally follow the contours of the groundwork. Once you have completely covered the area you can, if you wish, add further layers. One is usually enough unless

ABOVE Roughly clockwise from left back: Glass Etch aerosol, for frosting plastic surfaces to look like ice; Lightweight Hydrocal plaster, for casting rocks and adding layers over plaster bandage; Celluclay instant papier maché for basic groundwork, and FADS fine surface filler; Nimix Artificial Water; Artist's Medium gel (gloss), and Loctite Wood Bond Rapid PVA glue; plaster bandage; Woodland Scenics rock moulds; ultra-fine poly-beads for snow effects; earth-colour pigment for colouring Celluclay; Woodland Scenics Scenic Cement and Hob-e-Tac adhesive. The two plastic bottles, one with a black cap and one with white, are a two-part resin called Ultra-Glo from the Micro-Mark company in the USA; I use it to recreate water. It is very easy to use since you don't have complicated ratios of hardener to resin, you just mix it 50/50. The Rainbow cement colouring is just that - it's used to dye cement, so it's ideal for colouring plaster and Celluclay.

ABOVE The Field Grass on the left is from Woodland Scenics, as are the packs of Talus. In the centre is a block of rubberised horsehair; and on top of that a pack of sand from the German company Busch, which I found in a local model shop. Behind the pieces of driftwood is a strip of horsehair that you can get for making instant hedges; the two jars in the middle hold Deluxe, another type of resin to create instant water.

you are covering a very large area or have to bridge a fair-sized gap, in which case you will need to make some form of support such as cardboard or plywood formers. Make up your shapes and then lay the wetted bandage over them; wait a few minutes and it will be ready to take paint or ground cover.

Powdered plaster, on the other hand, is tougher and more suitable where you need some really solid scenery; this is the best medium for casting rocks. The type I favour is Lightweight Hydrocal, which has the advantage of working just like plaster of Paris but, as the name implies, the finished casting weighs only about half as much. In a fair-sized diorama this can be a serious consideration.

Snow Effects In the photograph on page 13 a small pile of 'snow' is just visible. This comes from the 4D Model Shop and is, in fact, made of minute separate poly-beads, so fine that if you tip the container they flow across the surface like water. This material is ideal for freshly fallen or powdered snow. (Do take care not to sneeze while applying it to the model, or to inhale with your face too near it - it is sensible to wear a mask while working with it.) Once it is in place, drift some hairspray across it to hold it down. Don't spray directly at it or you will just blow it straight off the model - hold the aerosol parallel with the surface and let the spray drift down onto the snow. If you're just adding a dusting, gently blow it about in swirls on the groundwork to simulate

the effect of the wind on powdery snow. Again, you can hold it in place with a drift of hairspray.

Other materials for snow include baking powder and, for slush, Alum BP - another material which you can buy at a chemist. Both can be mixed with PVA or secured with a coating of hairspray. To add a bit of sparkle to your snow, take some Alum BP, which is crystalline, and crush it to produce a very fine powder. Add this to whatever you are using for snow, and the light will pick up reflections from the tiny crystals. An alternative to this is to buy the packets of snow sold by Hudson & Allen Studio in the USA (see Appendix); this incorporates 'sparkle' in the material, and can be used straight from the packet. (They also make useful packets of Muck and Slush.)

For really heavy snow the best medium is plaster, added to water until you have a thick, creamy mix that will just about pour from the bowl. Pour it over your buildings, fallen trees, boulders, etc., and let it set. If you've got the mix just right it will flow slowly down to the eaves of a roof and then stop, just before dropping off. Even if some does fall off, it doesn't matter - that's what snow does.

Rock Moulds While you can make rocks by moulding plaster over formers made from taped-up balls of newspaper, the best results are obtained by buying some of Woodland Scenics' Rock Moulds. Made from heavy-duty rubber, these moulds enable you to cast a variety of different types of rock: stratified layers, water–smoothed river boulders, wind–eroded outcrops and many others. They are simple to use and the results are excellent. Just mix your plaster, fill the mould, and tap it on the table to remove any air bubbles. Once the plaster is set, simply peel off the mould, and you are the proud owner of a detailed lump of rock that would have taken Mother Nature a few million years to form.

Talus is the broken–up remains of rock – the slopes of scree seen on mountainsides are rock talus. Woodland Scenics make three grades: coarse, medium and fine. This pumice-like material is ideal for all kinds of broken rock, stones or gravel, and can be scattered amongst larger, moulded plaster rocks to great effect. It comes in two shades, natural and brown, but you can paint it with acrylics to change the colour.

The photograph on this page also shows some other items you can use for stones, including lentils and split peas. Both these are good for representing water-smoothed stones in the bed of a stream, but use them sparingly, mixing them up with a variety of other stones – they are usually of a uniform size, and too many of them in one area look very artificial.

Water Effects One thing to bear in mind before discussing the various mediums that you can use to represent water is that, before using any of them on your diorama (with the exception of painted plaster), you must ensure that you have securely sealed the bed of your pond or river, using layers of PVA or varnish. One useful product is E-Z-Water from Woodland Scenics. These are small pellets of resin; you tip them into a disposable tin can, and heat them on a stove until they melt. Don't heat them for too long or they tend to go brown. Once you have an almost clear liquid in the can, lift it off the heat with a pair of tongs and pour the resin carefully into the prepared depression in your model.

Another medium for creating water is two-part clear resin, of the sort used to embed items for display. Alex Tiranti is a useful source for this; he also provides a booklet on how to use the stuff (see Appendix).

Available from Historex Agents is an imitation water called Nimix. This is a gel which you melt down and pour into your river or pond, leaving it to cool and set. It comes in two tints, and the very faint olive green shade is the one I would almost always use - it is an ideal colour for almost any type of standing water.

A floor polish made by Johnsons, called 'Klear' (I believe this is sold in the States as Johnson's 'Future' polish) is an excellent medium to create puddles and wet areas on your diorama; but if you don't want to wait for ages for it to dry, only lay on a thin layer - it is not the medium to use for creating streams or ponds where you need any real depth. If you wish you can tint it with acrylic paints to achieve a muddy appearance; but it dries very clear and your groundwork colour will show through, so you may prefer to let this provide the colouring in your puddle.

If you don't want to get involved with resins or melting stuff down, represent water by using clear or tinted plastic sheet. Paint the bottom of the pond or stream in shades of dark and light earth colour, grading from dark to light as you move from the bottom out to the edges. Plant any weeds or stones you want; and then lay your plastic over the pond. Hide the edges by covering them with Celluclay or plaster and add some groundcover, reeds, etc., to bring the growth right down to the edge of the water.

WARNING I must point out at this stage that resins should never be used in a room with poor ventilation. The fumes of what is, after all, a fairly potent chemical can be quite dangerous, and anyone using these materials should not only ensure good ventilation but would also be well advised to wear a mask - these are available cheaply in many hardware stores. Children should never be left unsupervised by an adult if they are intending to let them use any of these mediums, nor if

BELOW The feathers at the back can be coloured a suitable shade and used for drooping foliage or some exotic jungle growth. The rear three piles are Woodland Scenics Talus in coarse, medium and fine grades. The middle row are a heap of ground-up kitchen herbs; lentils; and the meltable beads of Woodland Scenics E-Z-Water. In the foreground are split peas, and leaf-litter made from the seeds of dried silver birch catkins.

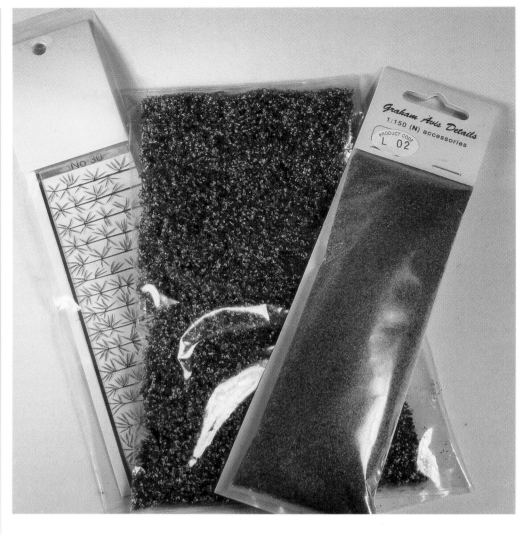

RIGHT Ground covers and etched brass bamboo from the 4D Model Shop. The centre pack is ideal for creating a heather effect.

ABOVE This flour sifter is just right for covering areas of your diorama with static grass or snow. The mesh is pretty fine, so it is really only effective for these two materials.

they are building a model using some of the more potent adhesives, whose solvents can also give off dangerous fumes.

Miscellaneous materials The accompanying photos show various materials which I sometimes use for foliage effects. Feathers can be coloured a suitable shade and used for drooping foliage or some exotic jungle growths. For the all-important 'ground scatter' representing fallen leaves and litter I have had good success with the ground-up seeds from dried silver birch catkins. The kitchen provides ground-up herbs - very useful, and they smell nice, too.

I use both bass wood and balsa wood in my models, usually for trees but also for large timbers; both are obtainable from most model shops. Bass wood is better when you want a nice smooth surface on which to work and to paint. Balsa is better for such things as tree stumps and hollow tree trunks, as it has a more fibrous texture and can be made to appear more lifelike. If you have to use balsa for something requiring a smooth finish, rub it down

with fine wire wool before painting or varnishing, as this will remove most of the fibres.

I'm well aware that this section of the book appears to be almost solely about Woodland Scenics products, and since they produce some of my favourite groundwork materials this isn't surprising. Contrary to appearances, however, there are many excellent groundwork materials produced here in the UK. The 4D Model Shop in London markets an excellent range of scenic materials under the title of 'Green Scene'. A company called Javis Countryside Scenics make various ground scatters, including a granulated cork which is ideal for fallen leaves, litter under hedges, etc.; they also market a very good tar macadam finish, as you will see later. Scale Link, initially best known for their World War I figures and accessories, now market a wide range of etched-brass foliage (see the 'Jungle' photos on pages 74–75), and also tree kits. I have tried to include as many of these companies as I can in the Appendix at the end of the book, as well as any other useful addresses.

THE BASIC GROUND

PLANNING YOUR PRESENTATION

Before you go to great lengths to create your diorama or vignette, it's worth spending a bit of time thinking about how you will present it to your admiring audience. I am assuming, at this point, that the finished scene will be built upon a rectangular baseboard. Most dioramas have one side which you have chosen to be the 'viewpoint', so a rectangle makes sense, but it also allows you to rotate the scene easily to be seen from another side.

Once you have decided upon the dimensions of your baseboard, get a piece of Medium Density Fibreboard (MDF) of the same size. Turning it upside down, fit a small 'foot' at each corner so that when placed on a table or display bench you'll be able to get your fingers under the edge to move it. If you intend placing it on a polished surface it would do no harm to get a piece of 'sticky-back' green baize and put a piece on each foot.

Turning your board right side up again, score the top with a hobby knife to give a roughened surface that will allow glue to get a good grip. Apply adhesive across the whole surface and then press your diorama baseboard onto it; weight it down with a couple of books or anything else suitable, and set the whole thing aside to dry. You can leave it at that if you wish, but once your model is built you might not be too happy with the raw edges of the MDF that will be showing all around the base. The easiest way to smarten this up is to buy some instant moulding from your local DIY outlet and, after carefully mitring the corners, to stick a length to each side of the base. Finish it off by either polishing or painting the framing.

The photograph below shows another way you can finish off your model. The baseboard has been set temporarily inside a custom-made wooden frame, which can be finished to taste. I am no woodworker, so I asked a colleague to make me this base in such a way that I could use it for any of the vignettes which I would be building on the same size of baseboards. It is made like a picture frame, and is rebated inside to form a ledge at the same depth as the thickness of my baseboard so the vignette sits level with the frame. A piece of hardboard has been glued underneath to brace the rectangular frame firmly, but a hole has been left in the centre of the hardboard so that, when I wish to change the model on display, I just push up gently from underneath and lift it out for replacement. When working on the model with the baseboard dropped into the frame I protected the latter with masking tape. (Any plaster that slopped over the edges of the baseboard when I was working on it out of the frame had to be pared off, of course, so that the base would still fit within the frame.)

This idea is quite useful for models of all sizes. If, like me, you have a limited amount of display space in your home, you can 'ring the changes' and display one of a number of dioramas at different times, rather like a picture gallery changing its exhibition.

LEFT The 'Slash & Burn' vignette from Chapter 6, set in the 'picture frame' display base described in this section.

ABOVE Even a bit of gravelly soil and a few ferns add realism to a small vignette, such as this Scimitar on the ranges - Salisbury Plain, perhaps?

PLANNING YOUR LAYOUT

Before you even start on your base you must sort out a number of points that will affect your choice of materials, paints, and so on. We must assume that you have settled upon a particular geographical area for your scene and some particular time in history. You now decide upon the time of year and the terrain. A spring or summer setting will call for a palette of bright greens and ochres whereas a winter scene is much more effective if you use greys, blues, blacks, and even a touch of mauve here and there - this gives it the necessary cold feel. If your choice is the autumn, then your palette will be comprised of shades of Raw Sienna, Burnt Umber, Burnt Sienna and Ochre.

Once you have a clear mental picture of the scene in which you are going to place your model, your next move is to look at the proportion of model to groundwork. Of course, the final size will probably be dictated to a degree by the amount of space you have to display the finished diorama; but you don't want the impact of your model swamped by the scenery - and conversely, neither do you want your Tiger tank hanging over the edge of the baseboard. It obviously depends upon the subject - a single figure, or the Retreat from Moscow. For a minimalist approach, see the photos on this page. This base is quite big enough to display a fairly small model, while the modest amount of gravelly soil and bracken gives a nice representation of a British military range somewhere in the Home Counties. Get the balance right; the idea of the groundwork is to suggest context, to compliment your model and act as a setting for your handiwork.

Decide upon the position of all the main components, and don't forget the angle from which the finished scene will be viewed. Placing your model bang in the middle of the scene, neatly parallel to all four sides, is the classic error; it will look much more interesting if it is set at an angle, and perhaps offset towards one corner of the base. If I were placing one or two Napoleonic figures on the model of the 18th century road in Chapter 10, I would place them towards one end rather than in the middle. The decision is yours; move the model around a bit and look at your choices before settling on the final position.

It makes life easier, when first laying out the groundwork, to make a rough sketch of where the areas of groundwork and the main objects are to be placed and then copy this onto the baseboard with pencil marks. They will obviously be covered up progressively as you work, but you can refer to your marks during the important early stages; thoughtful planning from the start means you won't be wishing you'd put the trench on the other side of the hill later on – a few pencil lines are much easier to remove than nicely hardened plaster. The first picture of the 'Firefly' diorama on page 44 shows what I mean.

CREATING THE BASIC GROUND

The base of your diorama will usually be wood. I don't use plywood since there is a real danger of this warping when applying wet plaster or Celluclay; my preference is for MDF, which makes a good, firm base. This is available from most timber merchants' shops, and you'll usually find that they will cut it to your finished size for you. I try to have a minimum thickness of ¼in (6mm) irrespective of the area of the model; and I paint both sides with varnish or paint to seal it (though this doesn't always work...).

I add layers or chunks of polystyrene ceiling tile when I need greater thickness to include built-up embankments, or sunken fox-holes, craters, gulleys or watercourses in the scene, using white PVA glue to stick the polystyrene to the baseboard. Should you need a really deep hole then a block of polystyrene is certainly the answer (see 'The Shell Crater' in Chapter 11), rather then trying to excavate a solid block of hard MDF.

Vehicle modellers often prefer to fix their models to the base with a small bolt or screw, particularly if they wish to give an appearance of movement in the suspension of their tank or truck. If this is the case, now is the time to mark out and drill the fixing hole, and then insert a small piece of rod to prevent the hole getting filled in during your landscaping.

The basic groundwork material will nearly always be plaster, Celluclay or some similar material. At this point you should consider adding colour to the plaster or Celluclay which forms the base coat of your diorama. Unless the base coat is to be completely covered at a later stage, it is a good idea to mix the appropriate shade of your soil colour into the plaster - anything from a deep black loam to a light sandy shade. This is worth doing so as to prevent the appearance of those glaring little spots of white which always seem to show up when you have finished the model.

There are several colouring mediums you can use. The most generally available are powdered poster paints, from almost any art supply shop, or water-soluble acrylics. The

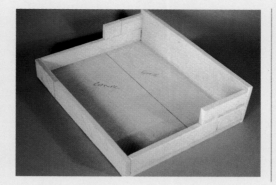

LEFT This is the box-like MDF base which I built for the 'Canal' vignette in Chapter 8.

ones I use for colouring the basic groundwork and for rock features come from Woodland Scenics. A few drops of pigment added to the water with which you mix your plaster will give you a good variety of shades. For colouring almost anything else in my scene I tend to use the Andrea Colour range of acrylic paints from Historex Agents. These come in plastic containers rather like small inhalers; their narrow nozzles prevent the paint drying out as quickly in the container as is the case with fully opening jars, so the shelf life is longer.

Now add your base coat to the board and work it in around any hollows until the board is completely covered. Leave it to dry; this could be overnight but, if you have a thick base coat, it could take several days. It is best to be patient - it is much easier to work on a firm base than on a treacherous layer of 'porridge'.

ABOVE A more usual type of baseboard and basic topography: the first steps in making the 'Napalm' vignette in Chapter 6. Pieces of polystyrene ceiling tile glued down to 6mm MDF, with Celluclay infill, make up the embanked base for this model.

BELOW This is the basis for the pond vignette in Chapter 8: a thick block of polystyrene has been hollowed out to make the shape of the pond, and the depression has been given a first coating of Celluclay.

ABOVE The real thing. An intricately fissured limestone boulder in central European woodland, tumbled from the mountainside above. Moss will grow in even the tiniest crack.

ABOVE These rocks, pushing through the scrubby turf of upland or moorland terrain, are cast in plaster from Woodland Scenics moulds, and set in a bed of Celluclay. The idea here is to show the rocks 'growing' from the ground, rather than sitting on top of it.

CENTRE A later stage, showing the addition of static grass and scatter for weeds and coarser growth. The rocks have been washed with Burnt Umber acrylic paint in such a way as to shadow the crevices and highlight the edges.

BOTTOM The finished vignette, with longer grasses and weeds added around the edges of the rocks. Remember that in any natural landscape growth of various kinds delineates the edges of things, where different surfaces meet.

CHAPTER 2
ROCKS, CLIFFS, AND A MOUNTAIN TORRENT

Rocks come in all shapes and sizes - great craggy slabs; layers of striated rock, tilted like spilled books; smooth, water-worn boulders; hulking masses of granite and limestone; wind-carved sandstone; cooled volcanic lava like swirls of solidified plastic - the variety is huge. Most of them emerge from the soil like the bones of the earth breaking through its split hide. While I do accept that boulders spilled down a slope do sometimes sit on top of the ground like discarded marbles, you still need to marry them to the earth underneath. Nothing looks worse than a collection of rocks scattered like an afterthought - like those elephant-grey rubber fakes dotted about on the sets of early 'Star Trek' episodes - with no attempt to blend the bases into vegetation or turf.

As usual, you must decide which are the most appropriate rock features for your model. Your model soldiers are not going to be simply 'generic' - so why should your rocks be? Match them to the time and place. The better they look, the more effective a backdrop they will form for the flash of colour and animation provided by your model figures.

If you are creating a scene from the Indian Wars in the Old West then there are many sources of reference for the wind-sculpted red outcrops and buttes of Arizona and New Mexico, which can range from a single pinnacle to something large enough to support a small town. If you're modelling winter warfare in northern Europe or the USA, then it's easy to find a travel brochure which will give you pictures of the snow-covered mountains. The rivers of the world carve their way down through the earth, and where they have washed for centuries the great plates and slabs of exposed rock are polished smooth by the water's action, and furred with bright moss. Above the tree line in the mountains you have slopes of scree, where rock faces have been reduced to fine rubble by interminable cycles of freezing and splitting. All these effects can be achieved with a little care.

THE CLIFF

To begin with the most challenging subject, I modelled a complete cliff-face vignette from top to foot - the type of setting which would suit a diorama of an ascent by British Commandos or US Rangers.

I used some different types of material for this model, in view of the size. If I'd used the usual MDF and plaster I would have done myself a serious injury when trying to lift it. To avoid this, I built the box-like base from foam board. This is a very light but strong board constructed of two coated faces with a filling of foam between, which I bought from the 4D Model Shop. I cut the profiles of the two sides of the box at the same time so that they would be identical; and then glued the sides, bottom and top to the back, using PVA glue and strengthening the joints with a second coat.

The next step was to fill the box shape with the basis of the cliff face. Since plaster would have been too heavy I used an expanding foam cavity filler from a DIY store. This one was by Polycell and called 'Polyfilla Gap Gun', but there are several other makes. I sprayed the foam into the box and left it overnight to set. In the morning it had expanded sufficiently to fill virtually the whole of the box (and looked vaguely repulsive).

I took an old bread knife and roughly carved the surface of the foam to the shape of the finished rock face. This done, I laid on two layers of plaster bandage to give me a good key for the layer of Hydrocal which I intended to use. I mixed up a bowl of this lightweight plaster and covered the whole of the rock face with it. Before it had completely set I took a sheet of crumpled baking foil and pressed it onto the damp plaster, creating a lumpy, fissured surface as the basis for the cliff.

While this was drying out I began casting a quantity of rocks, using rubber moulds from Woodland Scenics. Securing these with PVA, I gradually built up a craggy face; adding these extra features prevents an unrealistic 'all-in-one' look, and creates convincing fissures. I next covered the top and foot of the cliff with Celluclay; and when all was dry I gave the whole thing a wash of stone grey acrylic paint.

I used a mixture of different grades of Talus to spread around at the foot of the cliff, sprinkling it amongst larger moulded plaster boulders to represent the typical results of periodic rock falls. Rough turf and weeds have an amazing ability to root themselves on

LEFT The framework for the model cliff. This is made from foam board with an MDF base, so as to be fairly lightweight. PVA glue holds it all together.

LEFT The morning after: this is the foam filling, with its oddly unpleasant visceral appearance. It has expanded to fill the whole box, but despite the volume it weighs virtually nothing.

LEFT After carving the face of the foam to approximately the shape required, I covered it with a layer of plaster bandage to provide a key for the later work. You'll notice that I decided I hadn't extended the foot of the cliff enough, so I added a deeper strip of MDF board to the original base.

Once the plaster bandage had dried I added a coating of Hydrocal plaster and, before this dried, pressed a crumpled piece of kitchen foil into it to create outcrops and fissures in the rock face.

CENTRE RIGHT The next step was to cast sections of rock in Woodland Scenics moulds and stick them to the face. Once the main blocks were in place I filled in with smaller, random-shaped pieces.

BOTTOM RIGHT A layer of earth-coloured Celluclay is laid on the cliff foot, the cliff top and various ledges where I will be placing static grass.

almost vertical faces, and this was the next detail I added. Spreading small areas of PVA on a number of the ledges and outcrops, I scattered static grass over them and amongst the scree at the base. For the moss on a couple of the larger rocks here, I applied the tiny polybeads that I use for fine snow; once they were stuck to the rocks in patches I dripped on a bright green shade of ink, and the resulting 'fuzz' looked just right. I planted a spindly, etched brass sapling among the scree, and then turned my attention to the cliff top.

I first covered this with static grass and, when dry, stippled in a small path along the cliff edge, using an old paintbrush with a light buff acrylic paint. The gorse bushes were made from bits of a strange, spiky dried flower which I found in a florist's. I dipped them in

PVA and rolled them in a very dark green scenic material (meant to be used as foliage for fir trees). I added the gorse flowers with little spots of yellow paint. The tiny flowers in the grass on the face of the cliff are just that – tiny flowers; once again, these are from dried stems found in a florist's shop.

Most cliff faces are stained with water and salts leeched out from crevices in the rocks, so I decided to add a small area of seepage at the top of the cliff. I mixed some green ink together with gloss varnish and dribbled it down the rock face. After repeating this several times I touched the edges of the water in with a slightly stronger green to represent algae on the stone. I planted a couple of etched brass weeds in the crevice; and my lightweight cliff was finished.

LEFT Having given the cliff a first wash of colour, I began adding the small rocks and scree at the base, where they would have fallen over time.

LEFT Grass and weeds are being added on the rock ledges and in between the debris at the foot. One or two rocks have had moss added, made from the tiny polystyrene beads I normally use for snow, and coloured with green ink.

LEFT I have covered the clifftop with static grass, in which I have marked a footpath by stippling with an old paint brush, using tan acrylic paint. Note the gorse bushes, made from a spiky plant I found in a florist's, which I covered with dark green scatter before touching in the flowers with spots of yellow paint.

RIGHT A close-up of the water seeping from a fissure at the top of the cliff. I used green and sepia inks for the staining, and then dribbled on three or four layers of gloss varnish, making it run down the rocks as water would naturally do.

ABOVE Detail shot of the cliff foot, with a small sapling sprouting from a crevice and, on a ledge above it, a fern. Both these are made from etched brass.

RIGHT An overall view of the finished cliff after its final wash of grey-brown paint and the addition of various weathering streaks. I have also added little white flowers and static grass to the ledges. (Just a thought; but as I gazed at the finished cliff it occured to me that if the same method were used for a horizontal surface of fissured rocks, with gorse scrub poking out here and there, you would have a perfect setting for a diorama of either British, American or German troops during the battles on the hills above Cassino in Italy in 1944.)

THE GORGE AND TORRENT

The exercise here was to create a rocky gorge with a leaping mountain torrent, suitable as a setting for a Colonial American or Old West diorama. In my mind's eye I could see it brought to life by the bright focus of a British light infantryman's red coat, or by the figures of Indians and Mountain Men crouched beside the perilous 'bridge' of the fallen tree.

I had laid out the usual markings on the base for the relative positions of the rocks and the pool area; the rocks were then cut from polystyrene block and glued with PVA to the baseboard. Then came a covering of plaster bandage, which I find ideal for base work as it dries so quickly. (By the way, try to ensure that your bandage is fairly fresh; if it is kept for too long you'll find that it doesn't absorb the water very well and it won't be flexible enough to follow the contours of your base.)

Once the bandage was dry I added a layer of plaster and, before this had dried, I once again pressed a crumpled piece of kitchen foil into it to create a craggy finish. A layer of Celluclay was spread over the whole of the lower part of the scene, and then I gave it a coating of earth colour acrylic paint. Once this had dried I began casting rocks from plaster using my Woodland Scenics rock moulds; I added the larger ones to either side of the watercourse and some smaller ones to the bed of the river. I blended these in with plaster until I had achieved the outline shape I was looking for, and painted them using shades of stone grey and stone brown.

Another layer of pre-coloured Celluclay was then added, marking out the areas that would later be covered with grass. Colouring the Celluclay green helped to ensure that no nasty light spots appeared later on. I also added small areas of the green cover to some of the little ledges and outcroppings on the model.

Having laid out the grass areas I next painted the river bed with a shade of dark green, and coloured in the staining on the rock face where water was seeping down. I laid a central stream of brown staining and then edged this with a brightish shade of green to represent algae growth. I used water-soluble inks for these two colours, rather than paint, because I didn't want a hard edge where the two colours met and inks flow together very nicely.

The next step was to seal the riverbed, which I did by applying several layers of gloss varnish. It is a good idea to do this if you are going to pour any form of 'instant' water onto

LEFT The basis of the model: polystyrene blocks glued in place on MDF baseboard, temporarily set in a frame.

BELOW The blocks of polystyrene are covered with plaster bandage.

BOTTOM The whole thing is covered in a coating of plaster.

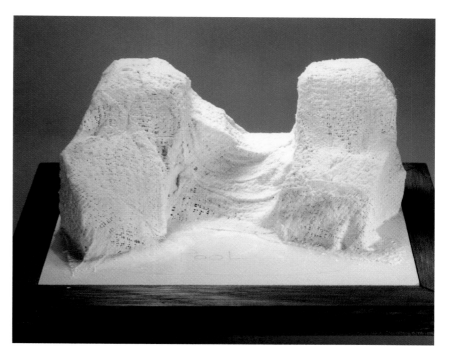

RIGHT I have added cast plaster rocks to give a more angular look to the scene. A coating of green-coloured Celluclay has also been applied over all those parts of the model to which I'll be adding static grass.

RIGHT The riverbed is painted dark green.

BELOW The real thing. Even where moss does not get a hold, rock surfaces are often spotted with stains and minute lichens in many shades - white, greys, browns, yellows and greens.

your model. Most of these are either a mixture of two liquids, such as resin, or they are a material that has to be melted before pouring it on. Nothing is worse than seeing your pond or river slowly disappearing down through the baseboard and spreading gently out across your workbench: I know - I've done it.

While the last coat of varnish was still tacky I added smaller rocks and stones to the riverbed. I knew it was unlikely that many would show through the final finish, but at least they were there if a clear spot should appear in the water. I intended to add a fallen tree to the scene, so I now made a shallow crater in the soil where the root ball would

have torn up the earth. Static grass was then applied over the areas of green Celluclay; and some etched-brass foliage was planted near the top of the two rock faces.

The water medium I used for this model was E-Z-Water from Woodland Scenics. Naturally, you must build a dam at each end of your river, and in this case I used plasticine stuck behind the two rocky bluffs and across the front of the scene. After gently melting the resin pellets in a tin can set on a stove top, I poured the liquid from the highest point so that it would flow naturally down the slope, and then left it to set. Now is the time to add any ripples or eddies you may want; just blow

LEFT & CENTRE A layer of gloss varnish has been painted over the riverbed, and extra boulders and smaller stones have been put in place in two stages. Water staining has been added down the face of the rocky bluff on the right; and I've started to scatter the static grass over the ground and rock ledges.

LEFT Some etched brass vegetation is fixed in place at the top of both bluffs; and I've made up the plasticine dams which will control the resin when I pour it on.

RIGHT The resin has set. Here I'm offering up the fallen tree to ensure that it is long enough.

RIGHT & BELOW The root ball of the uprooted tree is simply some Celluclay with short lengths of varying thicknesses of wire pushed in. Static grass and small stones were added to the top surface and the wire 'roots' were painted in varying shades of brown and grey.

across the surface with a hair-dryer as the resin sets.

As you can see from the photo above, the resin, once set, looked too smooth and treacly for the effect I wanted; but it was necessary to have this as a basis, since the stream at the head of the gorge would be smooth, with very little disturbance or foam, until it tumbled over the edge.

Once the resin was set I started streaking it with white paint, starting at the top of the fall. I pulled the paint very thinly over the resin so that the colours under the white just showed through, and added some very lightly applied streaks of plaster for foam. To create the

LEFT Close-up of the underside of the root ball in place. When coniferous trees fall they pull up only a shallow, saucer-shaped root ball, though the width will vary with the age and size of the tree.

LEFT The foam down the face of the waterfall is thin plaster, dragged out so that you can just see some of the green colour that I painted under the resin.

heavy foam over the rocks in the fall and the churning, foamy water at its foot I built up layers of plaster and then, just before it set, stippled it with a brush.

The final touch for the water was to add Artist's Gloss Medium over the pool and stream, and to push in ripples and wavelets with my fingertips. I left all the water to dry for a couple of days; then, when I was sure it was safe to do so, added several layers of high gloss varnish over it all, with the exception of the areas of foam. Foam glistens where individual droplets catch the light, but not with an overall glossy sheen like a body of water.

The fallen tree was from an old kit and did not need much extra work. I built up the base with Celluclay and then stuck in some short lengths of different diameter wires to represent roots, both large and small. The root ball and roots were then painted with a fairly neutral shade of earth grey/brown, and I stuck in some small pebbles. Static grass and some small stones were added to the upper surface of the root ball, and the trunk was laid in position.

ABOVE The boiling foam at the foot of the fall is made from several layers of plaster. As each layer was nearly dry I stippled the surface with an old paintbrush, until I had built up a sufficiently thick deposit. For the rest of the water in the foreground, I dabbed on layers of Artist's Gloss Medium and created ripples with my fingertips. This material dries almost transparent, so you get an impression of seeing through the ripples into the water underneath. Several layers of gloss varnish were finally applied over all the running water but only sparingly, in spots here and there, on the built-up plaster foam.

RIGHT For comparison, the real thing.

LEFT A detail shot of a photo-etched brass shrub, growing from the waterstained rock face.

LEFT The finished vignette.

LEFT For contrast, a detail from a diorama which I called 'Cave-Busters' (see also p.81 in Chapter 7, 'Jungle'). The cliff face was cast from plaster using a Woodland Scenics rubber mould, and then washed with a grey-brown mix of acrylics. The large leaves on the rock face are cut from a soft metal drinks can and stuck on with PVA. The rotten tree trunk in the centre at the foot of the cliff is a piece of driftwood, detailed with Milliput fungi; the ferns are all etched brass. In jungle terrain all rock faces soon acquire a heavy 'beard' of greenery growing in the crevices or looping down from above.

CHAPTER 3
GRASS & FIELDS, HEDGES & BUSHES

RIGHT Meadows left untended are not 'made of grass'; they are a lumpy, uneven mixture of dozens of kinds of grass and weeds of varying heights, textures and colours, often thickly dotted with wild flowers in spring and summer. Before the arrival of 20th century herbicides and petrol engines, most arable fields and roadsides were much more varied and multicoloured than they are today.

OPPOSITE This model of a Neolithic fishing village, c.5000-2200 BC, is one of six dioramas which I was commissioned to build for the Kantonales Museum für Urgeshichte in Zug, Switzerland. The scale is about 1/62nd - an awkward size, dictated by the display space. Between the huts and the wooded slope being cleared by felling and burning are vegetable gardens. Orderly rows of planting and realistic fencing can create a convincing impression of gardens of almost any period (and given the age-old tendency of soldiers to forage, these could make suitable settings for many military figures).

Most of the open countryside of Europe and North America where modelling subjects are set is covered with grass and bushes, or cultivated and divided by hedges. Yet modellers seem to find this most common of all types of terrain surprisingly difficult to render convincingly in miniature. The first trick, as always, is careful observation.

To take the simplest surface first - the variety of grasses, and the small weeds which grow amongst them, is endless. Very few expanses of grass look like a lawn (and if you look at even a lawn closely you will notice variations in colour). You can make a single patch of grass come alive by varying the colour, length and coarseness of the growth.

Since most of us model uncultivated areas or terrain that has been ravaged by war, you can also add weeds to the scene - and these don't have to be just little dark green bits of ground cover. Weeds grow to all heights and in many shades of green and reddish brown. Look at pictures of World War II bomb sites in cities, or at the aftermath of fire sweeping through any wilderness area: they are a mass of colour, with flourishing growths of deep pink 'fire weed' (rosebay willowherb) standing

sometimes to waist height. Before 1945 most meadows and road verges were heavily sprinkled with wild flowers in season. If you want to have some variety in your hedges then get hold of pictures of pre-war examples, which were often 'laid' - i.e. the heavy frame growth was partly cut through, bent sideways, and tucked into the next piece to produce a sturdy fence of natural growth.

The seasons also offer you a chance to vary the appearance of your ground cover, with bright summer colours giving way to the rusty shades of autumn, to the blue-grey shadows and tints of winter. I admit that I don't try to recreate accurately the actual appearance of a hawthorn hedge or a patch of wild primroses in my dioramas - I feel that some artistic licence is permissible, and the groundwork is, after all, meant to act as a background for your model; but if you do want to copy nature exactly, then there are a vast range of natural history books available for use as reference.

Reeds, tall grasses and standing crops are easily made with bristles; I find the best ones to use are from a cheap wallpaper pasting brush. They are usually a very pale tan colour, ideal to use 'as they are' for dead grass, and they're softer than ordinary paintbrush

ABOVE Using the metal tank tracks to impress the track pattern into the groundwork.

bristles. Planting them in the groundwork is best done using a pair of tweezers - just grip a small clump and press them into the plaster or glue. If putting them into groundwork that has dried, drill a small hole, dip the base of the bristles in PVA and push them into the hole. One effect of 'planting' grasses in this way is that they always finish up in a V-shaped tuft. Try to plant them so close together that this shape is disguised - or push them into the groundwork to such a depth that the sides of the hole push the bristles parallel. (I realize that this is not always possible, say when putting in a line of grasses as opposed to a patch.) Once in place, make sure the grass is not all the same length - trim it in a ragged fashion with scissors, and also leave some lengths of it lying at an angle from the upright stems; this helps to break up any uniformity.

Modelling this sort of vegetation is unavoidably time-consuming; but it adds a lot to a diorama, and if you want the best effects there is nothing for it but to persevere. Obviously, it is easier to summon up the stamina to tackle modest vignette bases rather than large areas of a major diorama.

TANK TRACKS

The depiction of tanks ploughing through deep mud is an effect that is often used in dioramas; so for a change I thought I'd like to

show the effect of a tank crossing fairly hard ground and dry turf, suitable for a model of Normandy or a Russian Front summer campaign. Again, this is very simple, but I find it best to lay your groundwork like the real thing - i.e a layer of Celluclay to represent the earth, and then static grass for the turf. Having applied the Celluclay to the baseboard I let it dry, and then misted the board with Scenic Cement. I made up a mixture of both green and straw-coloured static grass, and scattered it across the scene.

While this was still damp, I placed a 1/35th scale Sherman on the base and pressed it into the Celluclay to mark the width and gauge of the impression the tracks would make. I then made up a short length of Friumodel's white metal Sherman track, and pressed it hard into the turf. As the Celluclay was fairly dry the tracks made quite a shallow impression. I also added a piece of corrugated iron and a bit of barbed wire at this point, for a touch of local colour. I then cut back the bristles on an old paintbush and applied FX Mud along the track marks, using a stippling motion as with a stencil brush, to represent the torn-up soil. Don't carefully scrape all the static grass away - in real life it would be mashed into the soil. If you feel the track marks are a bit too indistinct when you've finished, emphasize them a little by pressing the blade of a screwdriver into the groundwork just behind each impression of a track bar, throwing it slightly into relief.

THE PLOUGHED FIELD

Wars throughout history have been fought across some poor devil of a farmer's fields, so with slight adjustments this would make a realistic setting for fighting men or machines of just about any period. However, I've chosen here to show a peaceful scene that might be found anywhere in the 20th century countryside.

The basic shape of the field is covered with Celluclay, the areas of the path and the bank being slightly raised by the addition of strips of polystyrene stuck to the baseboard. At this point I added a tree stump in the corner. Unlike the other stumps in this book I did not make this one from balsa dowel, but used a pre-formed plaster stump. Personally I like plaster accessories, as they take acrylic water-paints so well.

Once the basic shape had set I added the fence, made from bass wood strip and coloured with 'Weather-It' for instant aging (see Appendix). This is not a paint but a chemical that actually changes the colour of the wood and penetrates into it, so the more you add, the darker the wood. I next added the grass with Woodland Scenics Static Grass, mixing two shades to give the uneven effect of dead and live grasses together. The taller grasses around the edge of the field are made with Woodland Scenics Field Grass; this comes in packets of much longer lengths of fine materials for use as tall grasses, reeds, etc., made in a couple of different shades for use at different times of the year, Summer and Autumn. Don't try to cut these to the finished length if you are placing short clumps like these - it will drive you mad. Stick the clumps onto the base full length and then, once the glue has set, trim them to the desired height. Don't trim them all to same level; using the scissors at angles from the vertical, cut down into the clumps to achieve an uneven finish.

When gluing light, wispy material like this, I use an adhesive called Hob-e-Tac (yes, Woodland Scenics again). This is a very viscous, clear adhesive (with a very strong fume odour, so use it in a well-ventilated room). It comes in a glass jar with a brush integral with the lid. I normally dip the brush in the glue, touch the base of the clump of grass to the glue, and immediately put it in place on the model. This adhesive starts to dry almost at once, on contact with the air, so it holds lightweight ground cover such as clumps of grass upright almost as soon as they are in place; you don't have to spend ages holding it in position, waiting for the glue to

dry, as you would with your usual PVA white glues.

The ridges and furrows in the field were initially formed with strips of plasticine (yes, I know blue isn't exactly the best colour but it was all I had at the time). These were roughened up to give them some texture, to represent newly turned clods of earth. On top of this I added a thin layer of pre-coloured Celluclay, into which I placed some small stones to help break up any uniformity (not only does Nature abhor a vacuum, as my science teacher once said, but she's not too keen on straight lines, either). If you look at any piece of earth that has been turned up by ploughing, digging, or an explosion, you will always see myriads of small stones embedded in the exposed surface - a uniform expanse of chocolate brown is simply not realistic. (You might also see tiny fibrous roots and tendrils, but in 1/35th scale I don't really think it is worthwhile trying to model these - they would be so fine as to be almost invisible.)

Another point worth mentioning is the difference between a ploughed field in the

TOP The basic shape of the field has been formed with Celluclay over the baseboard and polystyrene strip banks. The plaster tree stump has been set in place. At first I made this post-and-rail fence from bass wood; I changed my mind later, and converted it to a post-and-barbed wire type.

ABOVE The first layer of static grass is scattered around the edge of the field, alongside the path.

RIGHT By this stage I have put in the long dead grass around the edges, and trimmed it to the finished height. The tree stump has been painted with acrylics, and I have strung the barbed wire - this is photo-etched wire from my spares box, suitably rusted. I have also started to scatter the litter along what will be the hedge line.

RIGHT This shows the addition of the layer of plasticine over the 'plough', churned up to give a rough surface on which to lay the top layer of Celluclay. Doing it like this saves you having to build up a very thick layer of Celluclay, with the consequent very lengthy drying time.

RIGHT The Celluclay has been painted with acrylics and a scattering of small stones has been added. The hedge has been added, as described in the text opposite.

LEFT A different angle on the finished scene, set against a crisp autumn sky.

20th century and the same field a couple of hundred years ago. With the introduction of modern ploughshares the soil looks almost as though it has been cut in facets, with flat surfaces reflecting the light. If you want to replicate this effect, 'plough' your field with a sharp blade, using it at an angle.

Once the field had dried overnight, I gave the 'plough' an overall wash of earth-coloured acrylic and, when that was dry, I dry-brushed a lighter mix across the surface to gain even more colour contrast.

I finished the vignette with the addition of a small hedge. This is made from rubberised horsehair (see Appendix) already cut into strip form to make instant hedges. I glued this to the back of the fence, and then coated it with PVA glue thinned with water. While this was still tacky I sprinkled it with leaf cover. These 'leaves' are, in fact, little seeds from the catkins found on silver birch trees. Collect these in the early autumn when they are brown, and dry them; once they are dry, roll them gently between your fingers, and

you'll get hundreds of these little leaf shapes from each catkin. I use them in practically any scene for which I need individual leaves; you can also make excellent 'ivy' with them, as we will see in Chapter 10.

Once the leaves were dry, I added clumps of horsehair to the front of the hedge to represent growth pushing through from the back, and scattered these with some more of my instant 'leaves'. At the same time I added scatter below the hedge to represent the normal litter of dead leaves and twigs which will always be visible under almost any hedgerow for about six months of the year, from autumn to early summer when new growth hides it. I applied a very pale buff paint to the path area, using an old brush and working it like a stencil brush, to give the appearance of pale, dried mud. I also used the same colour to dry-brush the grass to add to the appearance of a 'live/dead' mix of growth. Finally, a very thin coat of diluted PVA was sprayed over the whole hedge and path, and some more leaves were scattered over it all.

THE HEDGED MEADOW

Many show-goers will recall with horror various 'Normandy *bocage*' dioramas in which beautifully realised Sherman and Panther models are displayed forging through strips of giant salad made from lichen straight from the pack. Convincing hedges take care and patience, but amply repay the effort. This section describes a model of a rather more detailed hedge than the one in the previous vignette, and made in three stages.

For the purposes of this demonstration I have not attempted one of those great embanked Norman hedges, with centuries of tangled undergrowth and full-size trees

BELOW Yes, I know they look like rabbit droppings ... these are the pellets of Celluclay placed on the groundwork, ready to be feathered in to the top of the soil.

thrusting up from the foundation of a long-engulfed dry stone wall. My hedge is a peaceful field boundary; but the principles are exactly the same, and you could recreate the *bocage* by applying them to specific pictorial reference from Normandy in June–July 1944.

Hedges are not just simple strips of 'linear growth', but have a definite shape and frame. The basic framework is formed by the spaced-out mature stems, as thick as saplings, from which twiggy branches protrude in all directions. From these spread even lighter shoots and small twigs, and finally the leaves.

The bank on which my hedge is placed was formed by the usual strip of polystyrene glued to the rear of the baseboard, the whole of which I then covered with Celluclay. Into this I pushed some thickish twigs (from an old garden broom) to represent the heavy, mature growth that forms the frame of the hedge. Next, I scattered a mixture of material – the 'litter' that gathers over the years under a hedge – all around the base of these twigs and along the bank. This scatter was a mixture of ground herbs from a delicatessen (some herbs are exactly right for dead leaves), ground-up dried tealeaves, and a large dried leaf which I also ground to a fine litter. All this was sprinkled onto a layer of Woodland Scenics Scenic Cement.

I then added a layer of lighter horizontal and diagonal growth to the hedge, made from rubberised horsehair, to which I glued some foliage material; and finally a light sprinkling of ground cover in shades of green, to give varying colour and texture. All this was then given a final spray of Scenic Cement.

For the surface of the meadow in the 'foreground' of the vignette I rolled up some irregular-sized pellets of Celluclay and worked them into the groundwork in front of the hedge; such 'humps and bumps' are found in most uncultivated fields. These were feathered in to blend with the ground; then the whole area was sprayed with thinned PVA, and sprinkled with 'Rough Pasture' ground cover mix from Javis Countryside Scenics (see Appendix). You can, of course, mix your own multi-coloured ground covers from various different packs so as to achieve varying shades of green or autumnal colours – you very rarely, if ever, see a meadow or area of grassland which is all an identical shade.

Once everything was dry, I added a slightly darker mix to the 'bumps' to give the

LEFT The pellets of Celluclay pressed into the groundwork to make the uneven humps in the surface of the meadow.

LEFT The 'Rough Pasture' ground cover mix has been scattered over the meadow, and darker, coarser material has been added to pick out the tussocks. (If your meadow scene is set in winter, the grass on these hummocks could be longer, and a dead yellow against the washed-out green background of the field grass.) Pushed into the Celluclay on the bank, the thicker pieces of twig make the older framing growth of the hedge.

LEFT Before adding any foliage to the hedge I started filling in between the twigs with crushed leaves of rosemary herb and small cork chippings, to represent the leaf-litter found under all mature hedges.

LEFT Rubberised horsehair has been glued to the twig frame of the hedge to form the lighter growth, and then fine green scatter has been added as the leaves.

impression of rather coarser growth. Finally, at the base of the hedge, I planted some small flowers to add a slight touch of colour. The small yellow ones are made of wax and I found them in a shop selling doll's house accessories; the others are simply discs of paper, punched out using one of Historex Agents excellent 'Punch & Die' sets. The edges were snipped with a pair of scissors and they were coloured with acrylics. They aren't meant to represent any particular flowers, but in the scales to which most of us work they are perfectly acceptable. (It's worth noting that wild flowers are now re-appearing in the English countryside in larger numbers than for many years, since so many farms are now reducing or even completely abandoning the use of pesticides.) Most areas of grassland will have quantities of tiny white, yellow and mauve flowers growing in thick clumps in amongst the grass, and - in smaller numbers - others in blues, pinks and reds. If your diorama is set in pre-20th century times then the wild flowers should be found in even greater profusion.

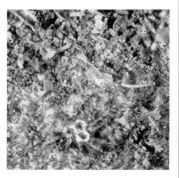

ABOVE I confess that these flowers - made from paper and wax - aren't supposed to represent any particular types; but they add a nice touch of colour to the scene.

RIGHT An occupant for the meadow, which is photographed here butted up against the woodland vignette from Chapter 5. (Horse painted by Charles Davis.)

THE SLIT TRENCH

During World War II almost every infantryman in the combat zone had to 'dig in' almost every night, usually in a two-man slit trench about the size of a grave; one man kept watch while his mate slept. Whenever circumstances allowed they tried to rig up some overhead cover over half of the slit - at least with their shelter-halves, to keep out the rain, and where possible with something more substantial to give some protection against mortar fire. If they were near buildings then any wooden door in the vicinity was quickly 'liberated'; the more serious veterans even dragged out chests of drawers and filled them with earth. British Tommies were particularly known for their nest-building instincts; if they stayed in one place for more than 24 hours they tended to construct cozy 'doovers' with improvised creature comforts. It occurs to me that modellers miss out on the possibilities this offers for rather more imaginative NW Europe dioramas; and this vignette illustrates a very basic 'slit' with hasty overhead cover in the corner of a Normandy meadow.

As I didn't have a block of polystyrene handy for this model, and I needed some depth in the groundwork for the trench, I built up the base by gluing five polystyrene ceiling tiles together with PVA and adding the bank at the back with a further strip. The next day I cut out the rectangle for the trench; this should be about 4 to 5 feet deep in scale, and if you really want to detail the interior then one end should be stepped down deeper than the other - this 'sump' was for water drainage.

I also decided to show the impact mark from a mortar bomb. Unlike artillery shells and bombs, mortars don't make craters unless they fall in very soft ground; on hard summer ground they explode upon impact without penetrating, and the blast scythes sideways across the surface, leaving only a shallow saucer-shaped depression some 9 to 12 inches deep and about six feet across.

I covered the whole base with a layer of earth-coloured Celluclay, building it into a slope so the bank didn't rise too abruptly out of the field. The resulting layer of Celluclay was fairly thick in places, so I left the model on a night storage heater for about 48 hours to dry thoroughly.

The next step was to cover areas of the meadow with a mixture of different green scatters and a few clumps of coarser scatter to represent grass and weeds, leaving the areas of the trench and mortar strike bare. I then took

some fine wire and a few pieces of my precious fan coral (see Chapter 5), and pressed them into the walls of the trench to represent fine roots that had been cut when the trench was dug. At the same time I added in some small stones. I repeat - it's important to remember that in almost any part of the world and certainly throughout Europe and North America, if the earth is disturbed by man or nature you will find thousands of tiny stones coming to the surface or showing in the face of a cut.

I now made the covering for one end of the trench. I started by making an old wooden ledge-and-brace door, still with its rusty hinges, and painted it in a nice faded pale blue. I knew that it would be almost completely hidden, but I always make any components for my dioramas as though they will be fully visible; that way I know that whatever does show will look right. With the door in place I also laid a piece of rusty corrugated iron across the end of the trench. I then made a few sandbags from Milliput and stuck them on the door - British infantrymen often carried a few empty sandbags for consolidating their positions. The final layer of earth and turf spoil from the trench was then added with Celluclay.

TOP The basic ground cover of Celluclay over a stack of polystyrene tiles, with the slit trench cut out of the top layers.

ABOVE Rough meadow cover is sprinkled over the field, and the wooden door has been made to lay across one end of the trench. Stones and roots have been added to the cut earth surfaces inside the trench.

RIGHT & BELOW RIGHT The mortar bomb scar is seen to the left of the trench. The rest of the ground cover has been added, including the brambles on the bank and the heavier growth along the edge of the field. The low 'parapet' of turves from the cleared lip of the trench has been added. A piece of rusty corrugated iron covers the extreme end of the trench; sandbags have been piled on the door, and turf and spoil forms the top layer of this improvised roof.

Most slit trenches had a small cleared 'ledge' around them, giving just enough room for the occupants to rest their elbows and their weapons and munitions. The turves from this were often thrown forward to form a low, parapet-like mound, and in this scene they are once again made with Celluclay. I mixed some of this up and spread it in a thin strip to dry. Once dried, I cut it into uneven rectangles and laid them around the trench, mixing in some loose soil as well.

Next came the vegetation on the bank; the large clump of brambles was made from rubberised horsehair, sprayed with Scenic Cement and scattered with a covering of fairly fine ground cover. The stumpy bushes to the right are made with plaster on wire armatures; then I stuck on some poly-fibre which, once again, was covered with green scatter. I used an old paintbrush with short bristles to stipple acrylic paint over the groundcover to create the bare, earthy patches under the bushes. The tall grasses along the foot of the bank are Woodland Scenics Field Grass; once this was in place I added some heavier growth at the edge of the meadow and at the foot of the bank.

The final details for the trench were provided from an old Airfix Multipose set: the Bren gun, two ammunition pouches and a water bottle.

I was unsure how to finish the base of this scene as the edges of the polystyrene tiles weren't very attractive; so I decided to make the front face appear like a 'slice through the meadow', and coated it with Celluclay before adding roots and stones embedded in the earth - see the bottom photo opposite.

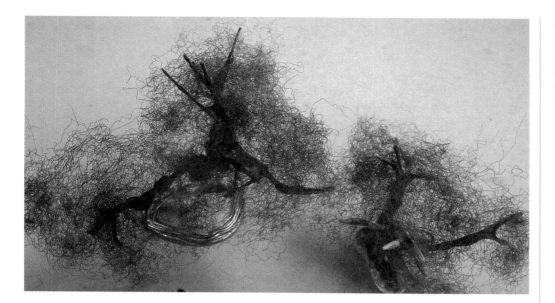

LEFT The final bushes under construction. The frames are plaster-covered wire, the foliage is poly-fibre, and ground cover will be added to make the leaves.

LEFT A view along the field, with all undergrowth in place.

LEFT The finished scene, with the Bren gun, two ammo pouches and a water bottle on the lip of the slit trench.

BELOW The embankment base
and the railway track are glued
and screwed in place on the
baseboard, which has been
marked out with the positions of
the main components of
the diorama. On the left the
majority of the embankment
has been covered in plaster
bandage; on the right are the two
last cardboard formers waiting to
be covered with masking tape
and bandage; and to the left of
these is the gap I have left for the
coal bunker. In the foreground is
the basis for the edge of the
muddy track, where I plan to put
a standing figure.

BOTTOM The whole model has
now been covered in earth-
coloured Celluclay, apart from
the railway track, where small
ballast stones have been added
from Woodland Scenics Talus.

THE FIREFLY DIORAMA

This diorama is larger than most of the vignettes in this book; the baseboard measures 12ins x 8.5ins (300mm x 210mm). I had already completed the model of a Sherman Firefly of 13th/18th Hussars on the Scheldt in Holland in October 1944; now I wanted a setting that would show it off. I find the contrast between the narrow Sherman hull and the long 17-pdr. gun barrel and rear turret overhang of the Firefly particularly attractive, so I wanted a reason to pose the tank with the turret traversed. The scene would benefit from a high feature to close off the back visually; so I decided to have my hussars halted for a brew-up under cover of the embankment of a secondary railway spur, with the gun traversed in the direction of the enemy. The embankment would also give an opportunity for some really challenging scrubby undergrowth.

I made my usual preliminary sketch plan, and marked off the main areas of the scene on the baseboard, drawing in the embankment, the track, and the coal bunker set in the embankment face. Next, I stuck down a strip of polystyrene as the basis for the embankment. On top of the polystyrene I added a strip of wood to which I had previously screwed two sections of Verlinden resin rail track. This track tended to curl up at either end, hence the need to attach it to the wood: glue would not have held it securely to the polystyrene. Once this had dried I cut out a number of formers from cardboard to make the shape of the slope of the embankment. This is one way of forming shapes such as hills and slopes without using large quantities of polystyrene block. Note, in the photo on this page, the gap left in the embankment for the coal bunker; it is easier to leave holes like this rather than trying to 'dig them out' later from the finished groundwork.

I stuck the formers along the face of the embankment block and covered them with masking tape. The next layer was added with plaster bandage; smooth the bandage down and leave to dry - this won't take very long. I repeated this for the area in the foreground where I planned to put a standing figure; and when it had all dried I applied a layer of white PVA glue over the whole. I didn't bother to colour the plaster bandage at this stage, as it was all going to be covered with coloured Celluclay.

The next step was to mix up an amount of pre-coloured Celluclay and spread it over the entire work area, with the exception of between the railroad ties: this was going to be covered with ballast. While the Celluclay was still damp I pressed the tracks of the tank into the pathway as a positioning mark for later.

I then added the first layer of grasses to the bank and the foreground area. This is Woodland Scenics ground cover, with a layer of fine scatter going down first followed by a scattering of coarser material for texture. Next came the rubberised horsehair to represent brambles and general scrubby undergrowth. This was gradually glued over the entire bank; a thin layer of PVA was sprayed over it, and further coarse flock and leaves were scattered over to form the final layer of growth. Long grass was added in one or two spots at the foot of the bank before the horsehair was stuck on in this area, and photo-etched brass ferns were strategically positioned. At this stage I also added the small stones between the railway sleepers along the top of the embankment.

Although it doesn't show up very well in the photographs, I lined the coal bunker with

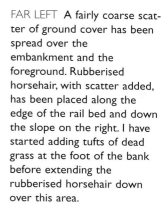

FAR LEFT A fairly coarse scatter of ground cover has been spread over the embankment and the foreground. Rubberised horsehair, with scatter added, has been placed along the edge of the rail bed and down the slope on the right. I have started adding tufts of dead grass at the foot of the bank before extending the rubberised horsehair down over this area.

ABOVE RIGHT Rubberised horsehair has been spread over the whole slope and covered with coarse scatter. More clumps of Field Grass have been added, and gradually the whole thing begins to come together, imitating nature's way of everything growing in a tangled mass.

CENTRE Puddles have been added with Johnson's 'Klear' polish tinted with ochre. I offered up the tank model to mark out its position, then built up strips of Celluclay mud pushed upwards and outwards by the tracks - it's easier to do this before finally placing the tank.

LEFT The finished diorama, seen from 'beyond' the embankment. Note the telephone pole, trailing wires, and rusty oil drum.

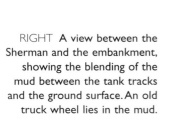

corrugated iron made from corrugated copper sheeting from 4D Models, and put in the heavy support timbers at the back and sides. When all were in position I 'grimed up' the whole bunker with black pastel chalk, and added some bracken around the edges. The piece of corrugated iron was also added in the foreground.

The track needed to be very muddy and wet-looking, so I made puddles in the mud by pouring on some Johnson's 'Klear' floor polish, tinted with a yellow ochre acrylic paint - my favourite colour for muddy water. I then added strips of Celluclay mud where the tank tracks have churned it up; while it would be easy enough to add this to the outside of the tracks after the Firefly was fixed in place, it would be very fiddly to try and get at the inside edges of the tracks under the belly of the tank. I then coloured in these strips of mud and blended them with the groundwork. More gloss varnish was sprayed over the whole base to ensure a good wet look.

Next, I went back to the bank and added the silver birch saplings - made from twigs from a garden broom - and a final scattering of leaf litter. I added some details, such as the rusty 45-gallon drum and the old truck wheel at the base of the bank. Once I had airbrushed a fine wash of black along the centre of the railway track to stain both the ballast and the sleepers, I added the telephone pole (for which I had left a hole in the groundwork) and its trailing wires.

It was now time to place the Firefly onto the base and blend the mud around the tracks, finishing off with another coat of gloss varnish. With this done, I placed the standing crewman and the final small details - a broken shovel in the coal bunker, and the British ration box, wine bottle, field stove, etc. beside the standing figure.

ABOVE An overhead shot of the undergrowth on the embankment. Note also the tank stowage, and the dismounted crewman standing by a 'Compo' ration box with a bottle and an opened ration tin.

LEFT The crew are dressed in M1943 'pixie' tank oversuits, here with the white/blue flash of the 13th/18th Hussars on the left sleeve, and black RAC berets. The 'Benghazi burner' was an old 4-gallon 'flimsy' petrol can, cut down and with holes punched in the sides to allow a draught; it was half-filled with fuel-drenched earth, and set alight. A second can went on top with water, tea, sugar and tinned milk mixed together. Many would allege that this concoction won the war for 21st Army Group.

CHAPTER 4
MODELLING TREES
(with Barry Bowen)

BELOW The differences between the barks of many types of trees are so marked that even in 1/35th scale you should be able to give a convincing impression: here, two of the many different varieties of oak and fir.

I should perhaps start this chapter by admitting the difference in approach between Barry Bowen and myself when it comes to making trees. He models specific types of tree; usually, I merely make a 'generic tree' - something which looks like a tree but is not intended to represent any particular species. This also applies to my bushes, hedges, flowers and any other types of vegetation that you will see in my models. I realize that my method is probably the lazy one, but I believe that the effects obtained should enable the average modeller to display his work in a reasonably realistic background, even if we are taking a bit of artistic licence.

Trees are probably the most difficult things to represent realistically in a diorama (apart from running water, and fire). To begin with, we normally have no choice but to compromise when it comes to scale. We have to judge the height that will appear in balance with the rest of our scene. Let's say that, like most of us who build military models, you are working in 1/35th scale, and you want to include a couple of mature beech trees. In real life a beech can grow to 60 feet tall; so you would need a model tree of just under 2 feet high (610mm). Even a silver birch, which grows to between 35 and 60 feet, would be at least 12 inches (305mm) high in scale. (If you really want to get carried away, a

1/35th scale giant redwood would be about 9 feet tall in scale …)

In view of these hard facts, you must either pick another scale to work in; stick to the smaller species, or very young trees, in 1/35th scale; compromise, and scale your chosen tree down; or model only fallen or broken-off trees. In this book the subjects of the vignettes were obviously planned for photography, so I have been able to limit myself to 'film prop' trees which end at the top of the picture, so to speak - see Chapter 5. (If all this really worries you, you could switch to making only boxed dioramas, where you would enjoy the same advantage.)

If you do want to achieve absolute realism and true scale, may I suggest you try to get hold of two books, either second-hand or through your public library. *The Complete Guide to Trees of Britain & N.Europe* by Alan Mitchell, published in 1985 by Dragon's World of Limpsfield, Surrey (ISBN 1 85028 000 2) lists practically any tree you could want, together with a description and colour drawing of the size and shape of a mature specimen, leaf shapes, their heights, and much other information. The superb colour identification plates in *The Oxford Book of Trees* by B.E.Nicholson & A.R.Clapham, Oxford University Press (1975), are particularly good on the differing

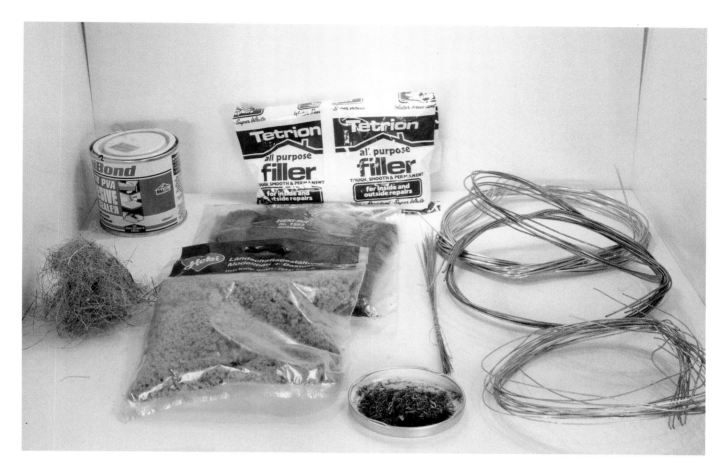

appearance of bark; but for modellers this book has a huge extra advantage. It includes a range of marvellous colour paintings of complete woodland habitats, showing not only which trees grow together in different terrains, but even the typical associated undergrowth and ground cover (the subjects are British, but apply equally to many North American and European habitats). Talk about being handed it on a plate … this is the sort of reference which could turn you into an obssessive.

Even at my own level, one can obviously model the difference between a conifer and a broad-leafed tree without too much difficulty, but personally I don't try to go far beyond that. The other difference that is most obvious between coniferous and deciduous woodland is the woodland floor, and surprisingly often modellers fail to spot this. In the conifer forest the floor is a thick, spongy mass of greyish-brown, long dead pine needles – and virtually nothing, apart from other conifers, grows in this acidic mould. By contrast, the deciduous wood has years of leaf mould piling up, rotting down and forming the compost for the seedlings of trees, shrubs, ferns, brambles, wild flowers, fungi, and almost everything else that grows on God's green earth.

Modellers whose personal experience extends no further than sanitised 'suburban' woods should remember that the ground in real wilderness woodland is also littered with fallen boughs and the stumps and broken trunks of old trees. In the wildwood, branches drop and trees are blown over all the time; after a few decades without human interference a forest floor can be a virtually impassable (and potentially deadly) maze of these deadfalls at every stage of decay, often entangled in undergrowth – and all the more dangerously chaotic if the underlying ground is rocky and uneven. Deadfalls, stumps, and the living trees themselves support mosses, lichens, fungi, ivies and other parasitic growths which add contrasts of texture and colour. If you are modelling a tropical forest you can add luxurious growths of creepers and vines to both the ground cover and the trees. Find yourself some decent reference pictures, and all of this can contribute to a realistically detailed and eye-catching backdrop for your models.

Of course, not all woodland is created by nature; mankind plants trees for coppicing, pollarding and harvesting. In the rubber plantations of Malaya and Vietnam rows of neatly grown trees stood on comparatively clear ground, allowing the passage of men and vehicles. Many soldiers have marched and

ABOVE **The tools of Barry Bowen's trade: PVA glue, Tetrion, packets of ground scatter, three or four different gauges of wire, coconut fibre, and, in the plastic container at the front, chopped-up pieces of sisal string dyed green. This last is for making pine needles and the foliage for fir trees. If you plan on using this method, you must ensure that you get** *sisal* **string, not the modern nylon type, as the latter will not absorb the dye.**

fought through orchards of fruit trees; and the olive grove is almost a trademark of the Mediterranean landcape.

As to the best way to make your tree, I personally believe that there is no finer mod-eller than Barry Bowen; one glance at his excellent models in this chapter should prove my point. The method he describes here is one that he has very successfully devised over many years of practice. It has the added beauty of needing no expensive materials: just some wire, plaster, PVA glue, flock, and a pair of pliers. If you follow his guidelines – of which an extract is reproduced here, with his permission, from his duplicated booklet *Trees*, which covers the subject in much greater depth (see Appendix) – then I am sure you will be delighted with the results:

MAKING A DECIDUOUS TREE

'If you have an ample supply of small or medium wire you can use this for your main frame; it is easier to handle, but it is rather wasteful if a heavier gauge can be used. The wire is used in multiples and twisted together, separated at a bough, divided and twisted again, and so on, working your way up. The amount of strands you twist together determines the thickness of the branch, and you will find if you can finish up with just one strand you will achieve the natural tapering appearance of the tree as it grows. Keep in mind that when you cover the wire frame with plaster, it will add slight thickness to the whole tree; so it is best to make your tree, the branches in particular, slightly under-size in thickness. You can always add a second coat of plaster to build up a trunk or branch if you find it is too thin.

'The main frame will be a simple tree shape and this method is best applied to trees over 8ins high. First decide upon the height of the tree you want, and cut your lengths of wire 2½ times the height you decide. If you have decided on a tree 16ins high, using 9 strands of heavy gauge wire, you will need 9 lengths of wire 40ins long. You can vary the amount, length or gauge of wire to determine the scale. Now to building the tree:

(1) Bend the 9 strands in half. You now have 18 ends together.(2) Hold the wires at the bend and make a loop large enough to fit three or four fingers (this loop will form the base). (3) Twist the 18 strands together; this section forms the trunk. The length of the trunk depends upon how many twists you make. (4) Divide the base loop into 3 groups of 3 loops. (5) Twist each loop and bend at right angles. You now have a base to stand your tree upright. If you intend to have surface roots coming from the tree, you could use a couple or more strands of your base wire separately to make these.

(6) Now for the top half of your tree. Using 4 of the 18 strands, twist these together for about 1½in. This will start the first bough. (7) Divide the same 4 strands in 2 pairs and twist each pair. (You should now have a forked bough with 4 single ends). The amount of twists will determine the length of the bough you are making. Make each bough slightly different in length. (8) Now continue with the trunk, twisting the remaining 14 strands together for about 1in; this extends the trunk. (9) Using 4 more strands, twist together for about 1in to 1½in; divide into 2 pairs; twist each pair for about 1in or so; and you now have

another forked bough with 4 ends. (10) Return to the trunk and twist the remaining 10 strands together for about 1in to 1½in. When taking out strands from a bunch, take them from different positions around the trunk. (11) Using 4 more strands, repeat as at Step 9. (12) Using the last 6 strands, twist together for about 1½in (this forms the last part of the main trunk). (13) Divide the last 6 strands in half; twist 3 together; leave 1 strand, twist the last 2 (making a bough with 3 branches). (14) Use the last 3 wires as at Step 13.

'You should now have 18 single ends at this stage, and you can shorten them back, if necessary …. You can now bend and shape to complete the first stage of the main frame. To make a tree with a double trunk, make up another frame, place them together, and bind the bottom 1in or so together; you will find this easier than making it in one.

COVERING THE WIRE

'A variety of materials can be used for this, but my personal choice is Tetrion. This comes in ready-mixed and powder form. The powder is best, as it can be mixed easily to any consistency. You can also add white glue to your mix to make it more pliable, but this is only suitable for trees with a smooth bark, and it also takes longer to dry. Mix the Tetrion in a bowl to such a consistency that when applying it to the wire, it is neither too runny nor too lumpy. Hold the tree by its base, upside down over some newspaper, and start to paint the mix onto the underside of the boughs and branches, working up the trunk.

'When completed, stand the tree on some greaseproof paper in a tray or dish, which you can use as a turntable, and paint the mix onto the trunk, starting at the base and working up to complete the branches. If you have surface roots, don't bury them in too much Tetrion. The only parts of the tree frame that should not be covered are the single, terminating ends (twigs). These are painted later, and if you are intending to add grasses as foliage, the ends will take the glue better if they are not covered.

'By the time you have completely covered the trunk, the top should have dried sufficiently to enable texturing. If not, let it stand for a few minutes until you can score it with a small, pointed knife. This is best done just before the Tetrion hardens off. Only the larger boughs and branches will require texturing to achieve the bark effect, not forgetting knots and hollows as appropriate. Using a small pointed

LEFT & CENTRE An example of the completed wire skeleton coated with Tetrion, which is then carved with the bark detail. Note that the ends of the branches are left uncoated, to accept the eventual cementing of the foliage.

LEFT The first wash of oil paint is applied and has soaked into the Tetrion.

ABOVE & RIGHT A finished model: the gnarled skeleton of an ancient oak tree. The close-up shows the massive surface roots and growths of moss on the bark.

BELOW & BOTTOM A smooth grey-green beech trunk contrasts strikingly with the almost 'netted' appearance of elder bark.

knife or stiff piece of wire, score the larger boughs with upward and downward movements, crossing over occasionally, to achieve the appearance of bark. After scoring, using an old toothbrush or stiff paint brush, stipple the surface all over, giving the tree a rugged look.

PAINTING BARK

For painting the trees, I find artists' oil colours give the best results. The main colours you will need are Burnt Sienna, Raw & Burnt Umber, and black. For the base coat, dilute the paints to a very thin wash with white spirit. Using a large brush, hold the tree framework upside down and paint as much of it as possible. Then stand the tree upright and paint those parts you will have missed. You will find that when the paint touches the tree it spreads out and soaks into the Tetrion, making it easy to paint and also quickdrying. Be careful not to make the wash too thick or the tree will look awful. It's a lot better to apply two or three thin coats rather than one thick one. When you are satisfied with the overall basic coat, you can shade the cracks and grooves using a small brush and a slightly darker wash; it sometimes helps to make this wash a little thicker.

'Here are a few notes on techniques and colours used on some specific types of tree: **Smooth Silver Birches** The bark on these trees is very smooth and mostly white. A thinned down coat of matt white enamel usually does for the base coat. The markings on the trunks and branches can be applied with a small brush, and the appropriate colours and shading in the forks with a shade of off-white. The upper branches and young growth are a reddish brown and for this I use Burnt Sienna. **Elms & Oaks** Use Burnt or Raw Umber for the base coat and shade with black, but don't overdo the shading.
Willows, Ashes, etc. Add a little white and a touch of green to the base coat to give a fresh, green wood look.
Plane The top layer of bark on plane trees peels in some places, revealing a lighter layer underneath. To achieve this effect, put small dabs of PVA glue on the bark where you want the light patches, and allow to dry. Then paint the whole tree in the darker base colour. The areas with PVA will appear lighter under the paint.

'If you make a complete nonsense of the painting of your tree, don't despair: just apply a fresh coat of thinned Tetrion, let it dry, and start again.

FOLIAGE

'There are a number of materials that can be used to provide trees with a variety of foliage … here is a list of some that I have found very satisfactory: various dried grasses and plants; coconut fibre; rubberised horsehair; sawdust; flock or scatter; soft drink cans; dried fern; dried fibrous roots; hessian rope or sisal string; silver birch seeds; lawn moss. All these can be used in various ways for different effects, as follows:

Dried Grasses & Plants These can be found in most good florists' shops, sold for dried flower arranging. Be selective and get the smaller-seeded types. These fine, small grasses are sold in bunches and are usually dyed in a wide variety of colours. Stick to the 'natural' looking colours – tan, shades of green, yellow, etc. These can easily be coloured to your choice, whereas the darker blues, mauves, reds, etc. cannot.

'In one bunch you'll find several stages of growth – loose, semiloose and tight. Sorted into their different stages they can be used for different effects. The very fine, loose grass gives a nice spring or early autumn look when painted the appropriate colour. The semi-loose and tight grasses make good late spring or summer trees, as well as being useful for weeping trees. The growths can also be varied on the same tree, thus giving the effect of a tree with a bushy lower half, which then thins out further up. These grasses are also used in conjunction with other materials, e.g. scatter, sawdust, silver birch seeds, etc. … added after the grasses have been attached to the wire frame. Some of the dried plants can be used to good effect for flowering shrubs and small trees. Gypsophilia and heather can be useful for this.

Coconut Fibre This can be purchased from upholsterers or can be found as stuffing in old mattresses and furniture. It can be teased out into different shapes and attached with PVA to your wire frame for oaks, elms and the like. Also, flattened out, pieces form the 'umbrella' shape for pine trees. It makes excellent hedges and conifers. Simply roll a bunch of fibre until you have the desired size and shape. Make a wire foot with one stand in the middle and glue the conifer to this spike. Paint the conifer with diluted PVA glue and sprinkle it with the appropriate scatter or sawdust. Let this dry, shake off any excess, and trim off any odd fibres with a pair of scissors. Using this method, you can make any size and shape of tree you wish.

Rubberised Horsehair This is obtained from good model shops and is used in the same way as coconut fibre.

ABOVE The foliage has been added and set with hairspray, completing this beautifully finished model of a mature tree in full leaf.

BELOW Foliage detail; the accompanying text lists a wide variety of possible materials for this stage.

RIGHT By using two differing grass heads, one finer than the other, you can indicate the difference between spring and summer growth, as in these two weeping trees.

RIGHT Your model trees can be scaled up or down to suit whatever size of model you wish, using the same methods; these were made to match a 1/72nd scale Milicast model.

BELOW One of Barry's amazingly lifelike models of a *bonsai* tree. Normally you would have to wait a hundred years to get an effect like this.

Sawdust Your local joinery company will probably give you as much sawdust as you want, at no cost. Grade it into fine, medium and coarse, using a sieve. When used with grasses it gives very bushy, fully clothed summer trees. Attach it to the grasses with diluted PVA, let dry, and paint the appropriate colour. Sawdust can also be used with coconut fibre and rubberised horsehair.

Scatter or Flock Also obtainable from model shops, it is sold in a variety of colours and grades. Use in the same way as sawdust.

Drink Cans Most drink cans are surprisingly soft and can easily be cut into sheets with a pair of scissors. These are used to make broad-leaved plants such as Palms and Yuccas.

LEFT The first three stages of the construction of a pine tree: from left to right, the wire skeleton; the wire covered with Tetrion; and the painted tree awaiting foliage.

ABOVE The first layer of foliage consists of chopped-up coconut fibre.

Dried Fern This is also sold by florists and is used for buttonholes at weddings. Try to get the dried and treated variety that is sold in large sprays and packets. This fern is used for fir trees with very good results. Break up the sprig of fern into varying sizes and attach it to the tree frame by dipping the ends in PVA and placing them in the desired position. Start at the bottom of your tree, using the larger sprigs, and work your way up getting smaller as you go, thus forming the 'Christmas tree' shape.

Dried Fibrous Roots These are the small roots to be found on dead plants and shrubs. Azaleas are a good source of supply. Once you have removed them, wash them and set aside to dry. Use these roots on winter trees to represent the fine, twiggy ends of branches; these are particularly suitable for oaks, elms and other such trees.

Hessian rope & Sisal string This fibrous material, when chopped in tiny lengths, makes good needle-type coverage for pines and cedars. To colour the rope or string, place a length in a bowl with a coldwater dye in a shade of dark green. When the dye has set into the material, remove it and leave to dry. Don't worry if the resulting material has a blotchy or uneven colour - this will merely give you the required variety in the shade of the foliage. When dry, chop it up into tiny pieces. Apply PVA to the framework of your tree and sprinkle with the 'needles'. Repeat this process several times to give a build-up of foliage.

Silver Birch Seeds Excellent results can be obtained with these when maple, beech, chestnut or autumn silver birch trees are being made. Paint them red and green for maples, copper red for beech, yellow/green for chest-nut and yellow for autumn silver birch.

Lawn Moss This is to be found in the long

LEFT The finished pine tree, with contrasting green needles - made from dyed and chopped-up sisal string - laid over the brown coconut fibre.

LEFT Detail of the base of the pine tree, with a 'cushion' of fallen needles and bracken.

grass of lawns. Collect several bunches, wash it and allow to dry. It is easier to colour this by dying; mix up a wash of green dye and dip the moss into it. Once the moss is dry it can be glued to the branches with PVA glue. You'll find this easier if you bend the ends of the branches to the horizontal, thus giving a larger area for the moss to stick to. Highlighting may be required, and this is done by lightly brushing the moss with a brush of undiluted paint. Scrub most of the paint off the brush and stroke it gently over the very highest points of the surface. A light green or yellow will produce the best results.

'All foliage is attached to the tree framework with white PVA glue. You'll find it easier if you let some glue sit in a saucer for five minutes or so; this lets the glue go tacky. Dip the ends of the grass, ferns etc. into the glue and then hold it in position on the tree for a moment or two. The grass is so light it will stick without too much trouble. Always work from the bottom centre of the tree, moving upwards and outwards. You will find that the lower, attached foliage will support that which you are attaching above, thus making it easier as you proceed. Apart from attaching the foliage at the ends of branches, put it into forks or between branches, creating new, small branches out of the foliage stems.

'Once the foliage has been fixed, the glue needs to be painted. In some cases a thin coat of Tetrion needs to be placed where the grass joins the branch before it can be painted.

PAINTING & FINISHING

Painting The two colours I use for the varying shades of green are 'Permanent Green Deep' and 'Cadmium Pale Yellow'. By mixing these two colours you can create most shades of green. If you require a really dark green, add a touch of blue. Mix your paints up in a jar and add white spirit to make a medium wash.

'Hold the tree upside down over some newspaper and paint the foliage using a half-inch brush. Then turn the tree upright, stand it on a plate and paint the topside of the foliage, using the plate as a turntable [see the 'Lazy Susan', Chapter 1 – Author]. Leave it to dry and recoat if necessary. To highlight the foliage, gently brush over the surface with yellow (not too thin).

Finishing After painting the foliage you will probably have spattered some paint on the trunk and branches, so it will be necessary to touch these up with the appropriate colours. At this stage you could, if you wish, apply a thin wash of green/yellow down one side of the trunk to look like moss. If you have used fine grass for your foliage, I usually give it a misting of hairspray - this helps hold it in place.

FIR TREES & PALM TREES

Both fir and palm trees have one main trunk, tapering as it grows. The basic trunk for both is made in the same way:

Fir Tree (1 & 2) Make a wire foot and trunk in the same way as for other trees, but use wires of differing lengths, twisted together - this will give you your taper. Finish with one single strand at the top. (3) Use 3 strands of thin wire together and, starting at the base, fasten them to the foot and then wind them up the trunk, making large loops at intervals … When winding up the trunk, keep the strand as close as possible between each loop. (4) Bring the loops out at right angles and cut each one. (5) Twist the cut loop to make a thickish branch, and when you have reached the desired length, stop twisting - the cut ends make twigs. (6) Coat with Tetrion and paint, using mid- and dark browns and adding a touch of Burnt Sienna for the reddish tinge in fir bark. (7) Add dried fern to the frame with white glue. (8) Dead firs can be made in the same way, but add short, stumpy branches at intervals to represent broken boughs. Once again, cover with Tetrion and paint.

'As always, it is best to get your reference from books and magazines to show you the various colour tones of fir tree bark and foliage. **Palm Tree** 'The palm tree described has a straight trunk, with all the growth at the top. Often these trees grow in clumps of two or three, which are easy to model using two or three main trunks. Once again, look for colour pictures for your reference. A palm tree trunk appears quite 'bumpy'; these bumps are formed where old palm fronds have become too heavy and have snapped off. (1) To achieve these bumps, start with the basic trunk (as for fir trees) and using one piece of medium thickness wire, start at the base and wrap it round the trunk, leaving gaps of about a ¼in on a tree of about 8in high. (2) Using another piece of wire of the same size, repeat the exercise starting from the opposite side of the trunk. This gives you a criss-cross look. (3) Twist these two wires together and cut them off, leaving ¼in protruding from the top. This will support your leaves. (4) When the trunk is covered with Tetrion you will see that the added wire produces the desired 'bumpy' appearance. More Tetrion should be added to the base of the tree, as this is usually thicker and smoother due to erosion.'

LEFT Detail from one of Barry's many vignettes, with a pair of coconut palms. The pirate figure is 100mm, to give you an idea of the scale of the trees. Notice the ripening coconuts - green, with a groove running around them, not brown and hairy as we see them in the shops.

LEFT One way to make palm fronds. These are leaves from a cheap silk flower. Pull the vein detailing off the back and stick the leaf to a piece of wire.

Cut the leaf into fronds with a sharp pair of scissors, and bend the wire stem to the angle you want.

LEFT These spiky tropical growths have been made from the spare sprue around etched brass plants from Scale Link. Cut the sprue into short lengths, trim one end to a point, bend to shape and glue them into the stem.

CHAPTER 5
AN AUTUMN WOOD

This vignette is an exercise in the creation of a woodland setting with convincing miniature trees, of my 'generic hardwood' species (*phoneyarbor windrowiana?*), on the basis of balsa dowel rather than a wire armature. As the accompanying photos make clear, the trees were always going to be strictly 'film prop' jobs. In other words, as the vignette was to feature the detailing of a forest floor, and the final photos would be taken at a low level, I didn't finish the trees off to the crown; but I hope this won't detract from the final effect too much.

Using 19mm balsa dowel, I built the basic armatures of three large, mature trees. I only took them as far as the basics, as I needed to build up the groundwork next to see how I would position them. I covered the baseboard with a thick layer of Celluclay mixed with water which I had coloured with Burnt Sienna acrylic paint. I left a clear strip where my muddy stream would flow and, after pressing the tree bases into the Celluclay so as to mark their position, I left it to dry for about a week. This may seem excessive, but it really is necessary when you lay down such a thick layer of Celluclay - it takes a long time to dry right through. You can help it along by placing it over a source of gentle, indirect heat such as a night storage heater.

In the interim I got back to the trees. I wanted trunks with a fairly rough-textured bark, so I covered the balsa with Flexibark. Obviously not all trees have such a rough surface - look at beech trees or birches; so don't automatically use this covering for all your trees. Beeches and other smooth-barked species can be coated with Tetrion or ordinary plaster and smoothed with a wet brush to achieve the right finish.

The next step was the addition of the branches. The thickest boughs are balsa dowel, attached with PVA. The thinner branches are made from a slightly unusual medium. Some years ago, when turning out an attic, I came across some strange pieces of what I thought to be some kind of dried flower, but they turned out to be fan coral. I believe it is now impossible to buy coral since it is an endangered and protected species, so I have been hoarding these ever since - it is an ideal material for twisty branches. I drilled holes in the balsa dowel and glued these boughs into place, covering them in turn with Flexibark. The next job, once the basic groundwork had dried, was to place the trees and, using Celluclay, to 'feather' them seamlessly into the ground. When this was secure I turned to the foliage. I used PVA to stick teased-out pieces of Woodland Scenics poly-fibre to the

LEFT The trees and stump are painted with a grey-green mix of acrylics; the barbed wire fence is in place at the back of the scene; and the stream bed is painted with a khaki colour.

LEFT Here I have started adding the foliage to the trees, using polyfibre and a medium green ground cover as 'scatter'.

LEFT The real thing - a hardwood forest floor in autumn. Notice the overall covering of dead leaf litter, the black rotten twigs, and the bright seedlings of this year's growth pushing through.

ABOVE Some of the material I used for the heavy leaf litter in the vignette. This is an old leaf that I dried out and ground up with a pestle and mortar. Before using the resulting mix I took out the thin, fibrous remains of the leaf veins.

RIGHT The tree foliage is finished, and the heavy leaf cover has been spread across the base. This is a mixture of my ground-up dried leaf and silver birch catkin seeds. I have also spread the first layer of gloss varnish over the stream bed, and dropped in some 'floating' leaves. The fallen boughs are now fixed in place.

BELOW Detail of the fungus on the tree stump. I made this from Duro, and coloured it with Windsor & Newton sepia ink.

branches; then, having sprayed this with Scenic Cement, I added a coating of fine ground cover.

I wanted a large fallen bough in the scene, so I used a bit of twig glued into one end of a small piece of balsa dowel. Once this was firmly set I used my Dremel motor tool with a ball-headed cutter to hollow out the other end of the piece of dowel, as though it were rotten, and covered the whole thing with a light coating of Flexibark. This done, I took a plaster tree stump and a sawn-up piece of tree trunk and, together with my fallen bough, I placed them on the model to check their relative positions. Happy with this, I glued the tree stump in place and feathered it into the ground with Celluclay.

I mixed up a grey-green colour for the trees and stump and painted them with a fairly wet solution, which soaked well into the Flexibark coating. With this dry, I dry-brushed the rough texture of the Flexibark with a paler shade of the grey-green; and dusted patches of green pastel chalk onto the trunks to represent areas of the bright green moss and lichen you find on old trees, especially in damp woodland.

I felt I needed something to draw a finishing line across the back of the model; so I made up, a barbed wire fence, using matchsticks for the posts, treated with Weather-It to achieve an aged, unpainted finish to the wood, before adding some photo-etched barbed wire coated a suitable rusty colour. I made another fallen bough from twig and laid it across the fence, dragging the wire down under its weight and pulling a couple of the posts out of the vertical. (By the way, many arts and crafts shops sell large bags of matchsticks for those modellers who build things like galleons and St Paul's Cathedral out of them. These naturally come without a striking head, and are very useful for all kinds of bits of timber; an inexpensive bag will last you for years.)

I next painted the bed of the diagonal stream a shade of dark earth and then, before the first coat had dried, worked in swirls of a

ABOVE The moss on the fallen branch is made from the tiny poly-beads sold by the 4D Model Shop for snow effects, but here coloured with green inks. In front of the branch tiny toadstools, made from Milliput, sprout from the rich loam.

LEFT The ferns are in position along the fence line; these are Scale Link etched brass leaves, as are the tiny fresh green shoots poking up through the litter, coloured with Humbrol enamels.

ABOVE The completed vignette. (I chickened out of trying to make a 1/35th scale squirrel to finish it off).

light tan colour and added some leaf litter. Then I applied several coats of gloss varnish for the water, not forgetting to add some more floating leaves into the last coat – in autumn woodland dead leaves cover absolutely every surface until they are blown or swept away. The vari-coloured swirls of brown acrylic I had painted on at first now looked like sediment moving in the water. Once the stream was finished, I left it to become completely dry before moving on to the next step, which was adding the leaf litter to the floor of the wood.

The litter was made from my favourite leaf material, silver birch catkin seeds. I sprayed Scenic Cement over the base and then scattered liberal quantities of the litter, misting another coat of adhesive over this first layer to secure it. When it was dry I repeated the process. When 'flooring' an autumn diorama, remember that fallen leaves come in a huge range of colours – from lime green to lemon yellow, through gold, ochre, orange, red, and every shade of brown to dead black – so you can mix your own litter to match your references.

Next I placed the fallen boughs in position, securing them in place with PVA. The moss on the large bough was created by sticking on some of the very fine poly-beads that I use for powdered snow, and then dripping two shades of green ink onto it, the lighter shade for the thinner growth at the edge of the patch and the darker in the centre; the addition of the ink tended to make the beads clump up into a more convincing mossy growth.

Now I added that year's fresh, new growth pushing through from beneath the leaf mould, and the ferns growing under the barbed wire fence. The new seedlings and baby saplings and the ferns were all from photo-etched brass sets which are made by Scale Link. While these were still attached to their frets I undercoated them with Halford's Grey Car Primer, and then used Humbrol enamels for the shades of green, finishing by coating them all with matt varnish. Once they were dry I drilled small holes in the base and secured them all with Superglue. The toadstools growing by the fallen bough were made from Milliput by my wife (who has a thing about modelling toadstools!) and tinted with acrylic paints. And that was that; apart from making scrunching sound-effects, I couldn't think of anything else to add.

ABOVE & LEFT The aftermath of an autumn storm outside an early medieval village (c400-800 AD) - another of the 1/62nd scale dioramas commissioned by the Cantonal Early History Museum at Zug, Switzerland. The detail shows a hunter venturing into the birch woods. The trees in this case were 'ready-mades' from an architectural model supplier in the USA; they were made of some kind of latex over wire armatures, with ground-up rubber foliage. At this small scale I only had to add the odd finishing touches with paint and scatter.

RIGHT The real thing: detail of moss growing on an old bough that has lost all its bark; note the silvery appearance of the wood, with dark streaks and insect holes.

RIGHT The butt of a tree felled with a chainsaw. Chainsaws were widely used for clearing landing zones in Vietnam, but pre-1945 trees and stumps should definitely not show this effect. Think about the ways in which axes and gang-saws were actually used to notch and cut through treetrunks before shaping your stumps and butts.

ABOVE Dead branches cluttering the floor of a mixed forest of coniferous and hardwood trees.

LEFT An old coniferous deadfall in mixed woodland, showing the remains of a broad root ball. In the right background note the heavy growth of bright green moss up one (the southern?) side of a hardwood treetrunk.

LEFT The trunk of the old dead fir tree, with the remains of bark scabbing off the rotten trunk, which is straw-coloured and lightly stained with green.

CHAPTER 6
SCORCHED EARTH

Military modellers often wish to simulate fire effects - or more usually, the aftermath of fire. A burnt-out vehicle or house is a useful visual shorthand which immediately establishes that this is a battlefield. Modern warfare isn't the only arena in which you would find 'scorched earth', of course. In ancient and medieval days an attacking army would routinely harry the enemy's lands, burning crops and villages, running off livestock and killing the wretched peasantry; in this way they destroyed the enemy's economy, and hoped to provoke him to come out of his strongholds and offer battle. During the centuries of black powder warfare the smouldering wads from musket and cannon often started fires in the dry campaigning months of summer - notoriously, during the bloody Battle of the Wilderness in May 1864, where thousands of Union and Confederate wounded perished horribly in massive forest fires.

The purpose of the next two models was to show the difference between land that has been burned off deliberately with the intent of clearing it for agriculture, and land that has been scorched by war. Throughout the centuries and all across the world, farmers would normally cut down the trees, separate the timber that might be of use later on, and burn the smaller branches; a certain order is apparent in such scenes - whereas in warfare, everything goes. If you look at a picture of a burnt-out tank you will see that around the hulk the earth is completely blackened, without a scrap of grass left, only white and grey ash. As your eye moves further away from the seat of the fire you will see that the scorching becomes gradually less severe, until on the very edge of the area the grass will only have been singed to a light brown colour.

RIGHT The initial construction of the base is illustrated on page 19. This is the polystyrene and Celluclay groundwork after I had sprayed it with a random pattern of matt black and grey acrylics, and added two layers of coarse scatter. The colours are all neutral in this model, so as to add to the desolate appearance of the scene.

RIGHT Rubberised horsehair represents burnt undergrowth; this has also been touched in with both matt black and grey. I've started adding small spots of white ash at this stage - this is just white pastel chalk.

FAR LEFT Working on the burnt-out tree stumps. These are made from the stems of a dried plant which had a very soft, pithy centre that was easy to hollow out. Once I had shaped them I added roots made from Duro epoxy putty.

LEFT Having attached the stumps with PVA I painted them matt black, and added some more coarse scatter around the base and in amongst the roots.

NAPALM

The first vignette represents a track through a lightly wooded area which has been ravaged by fire. I called it 'Napalm', but the same effects would suit a burnt-out area from the American Civil War or any other conflict in history.

The terrain was built up on the baseboard in the usual way, using polystyrene and Celluclay; and then airbrushed with shades of grey and black acrylic paints. Next, a layer of coarse ground cover was glued on, scattered in a fairly random fashion. Rubberised horsehair was used for the burnt-out undergrowth, and this in turn was also sprayed with black and grey. I used ground-up white pastel chalks to add patches of ash. The burnt trees were then made with twigs taken from the old garden broom and sprayed matt black. These were put in position by simply pushing them into the polystyrene base. I next added more burnt undergrowth and a few fallen, charred branches.

For the foreground I made a couple of burnt-out, hollowed tree stumps. Drilling out short lengths of a dried stalk that I'd found in a florist's shop, I made up the root system with Duro putty. They, in turn, were sprayed matt black and glued to the base with PVA. I added some more white pastel chalk powder to the inside of the stumps, and then touched in a couple of glowing embers on the lip of the bark. To get this 'fire glow' effect you need to paint on a small dab of white and let it dry. Next get hold of some Humbrol 'Day-Glo' paint, as used by the aircraft-modelling guys. Apply this over the white undercoat and leave to dry. Have a look at the effect when the Day-Glo has dried and, if it is a bit pale, add another layer. The white undercoat helps throw the Day-Glo up; and if you apply this on a matt black or shadowy area of your model it stands out very effectively.

(I must confess that I never attempt to portray smoke or flames in my models. I know it has been done with both teased-out cotton wool and nylon wadding, but it is almost impossible to create convincing gases or vapours without the much greater control allowed by a boxed diorama with directed lighting effects - so normally I'd rather not bother. But see page 73.)

A final dusting over with both grey and white pastel powder gave the model a nice overall 'ashy' finish.

BELOW Detail of the finished stumps. The glowing ember was created by painting on a drop of matt white and, when dry, overlaying this with a drop of Humbrol 'Day-Glo'. There are two shades of this paint available, orange and pinky-red - I used the latter.

RIGHT A fairly light exposure of the finished groundwork, to show the undergrowth, ground scatter and fallen branches. A fire moving fast through woodland sometimes chars but does not completely destroy tough undergrowth like brambles.

RIGHT A shot more focused on the skeletal burnt-out trees, made from natural twigs painted matt black and touched in lightly with greyish-white pastel chalk 'ash' details.

ABOVE Overall view of the
finished vignette from the side.

LEFT Surveying the damage.
Roy Dixon kindly painted the
Vietnam GI figure for me.

SLASH & BURN

The second model represents an area of cultivated land that is being enlarged by burning off the natural growth.

I started off with the field, making this from a Celluclay base and marking in small furrows. Next I made a number of tree stumps from balsa dowel. I modelled these as though they had been felled with a saw, cut at a slight angle and with the characteristic fringe of splintered bark where the trunk broke away from the stump as it fell. I covered the balsa dowel with a skin of Duro two-part epoxy putty, and scribed in lines for the bark before it set. In the photos I've shown two ways to treat the stumps: one merely has a ring of putty around the base, which is feathered into the stump to make it a bit wider but without any visible root system. The second has individual spurs of putty smoothed onto it so as to have a few gnarly roots showing above ground. Once they had dried, I coloured the

stumps with a wash of grey-green acrylic and then ran a thinner wash of a darker shade into the crevices in the bark. When all was finished I stuck them down with PVA, sprayed the area around them with thin Woodland Scenics glue, and scattered on static grass.

The next move was to create the area of scorched ground under and around the bonfire. I coloured this with matt black paint where the grass was completely burnt, and then faded that into a shade of Burnt Sienna to give the look of grass that was just scorched but not charred.

Fires such as **campfires** (another popular modelling scenario) and bonfires are basically made the same way. The logs are unburnt at the outer edge, and as they get closer to the centre of the fire they should be coloured gradually through shades of black, grey, white, a hot red near the ends, and finally a pale yellow to indicate the hottest part of the fire. White ash builds up in the centre and grey ashes and bits of burnt twigs form an outer ring. I have suggested hot embers rather than burning wood, and for this the Humbrol 'Day-Glo' is best.

When modelling a campfire it looks better to lay down a ring of logs with their ends meeting at the centre of the fire - this gives an appearance of deliberate organisation rather than simply destruction. Another type of cooking fire was made by laying two large logs parallel on the ground and about a foot apart, and building a fire between them with smaller fuel. This confined the fire; provided support for improvised grills and spits; and started the large logs on a slow process of smouldering, which would later provide a level of warmth during the night.

For bonfires just a random pile of wood or branches will suffice. A scattering of white pastel chalk was put on the spot where I would place the bonfire to represent the heavy ash layer under a fire, and one of the tree stumps was painted black and then 'charcoaled' on the nearest side to the fire. This is to represent the shiny appearance of heavily charred wood, and is simply done by lightly brushing graphite (from a 6B pencil) over the bark with your fingertip. This done, it was time to build the bonfire, made from small twigs from the garden. I painted a couple of areas of hot embers in the base of the fire using Humbrol 'Day-Glo', and then added matt black coloured twigs on top, with a few unburnt ends in the upper and outer areas.

I used some Woodland Scenics grasses and some very fine dried flower stems to create

LEFT The stumps have been painted and the first layer of static grass has been scattered around them.

LEFT The burnt area has been undercoated in matt black, with the edges of the grass and the face of the stumps tinted with Burnt Umber to represent scorching rather than burning. The nearest stump is completely burnt on one side, and 'charred' by rubbing over the black paint with graphite from a very soft pencil. A heavy white ash deposit has been placed where the bonfire will be sited.

LEFT A side view of the almost completed vignette. Leaf litter - from ground-up catkin seeds and the herb thyme - has been added all over the grassed area; weeds grow up around the stumps; the bonfire is in place, with a pile of twigs dumped beyond it ready to be thrown on the fire, and on the right a stack of logs saved for later use.

ABOVE & BELOW Two angles on the finished model, with an axe from a Historex tool set left stuck in a stump. The crops in the field are made with tiny dried flower stems. Note the heavy scatter of ash, burnt leaves and tree chippings all over the ground around the fire and the stumps.

ABOVE A close-up of the bonfire, showing the glowing Day-Glo embers underneath. This way of modelling hot coals is just as effective when used for campfires, coals in stoves, etc.; it is best seen through a partial 'screen' of bits of wood or coal so that it is partly in shadow, rather than sitting on top of a fire.

some growth around the tree stumps. I also sprayed the area with thin PVA onto which I scattered leaves and litter made with ground-up herbs, tiny pieces of cork and some catkin leaves. I added a stack of 'flick' (twigs and very thin branches) lying ready to be burnt on the fire; and a pile of useful lengths of timber have been saved and stacked by the stumps.

The crop in the field is made from some odd plants from a dried flower shop – I haven't a clue what they are but they work! (It is always worth while checking in this type of shop and

garden centres. You never know what you'll find that will come in handy one day.) When I'd finished gluing the crop in place with Hob-e-Tac adhesive I scattered a very fine brown flock over the whole area to kill any highlights from the dried glue; Hob-e-Tac sometimes leaves gloss patches when it dries. At the end of the field nearest the fire I added some bits of grey flock into the sooty grass, to represent shrivelled leaves from the crop. For a final touch I took an axe from a Historex tool pack and stuck it into one of the stumps.

ABOVE Detail from one of the commissioned 1/62nd scale dioramas for the Cantonal Early History Museum at Zug, Switzerland. This Bronze Age village scene (c2200 - 800 BC) was to be displayed with controlled 'night time' lighting and fibre optic effects. To recreate the findings of an actual archaeological discovery, the scenario was to be a thunderstorm during which lightning has struck one of the houses; villagers gather their animals and flee to safety while a group of men pull burning roof timbers down in a vain attempt to stop the fire spreading.

The burnt-out house (upper left) is made from wooden barbecue skewers, 'chewed up' with a pair of pliers and painted matt black. A bundle of optic fibres were secured under the model and led up through a hole in the middle of the ruined house.

The ends were tinted with orange ink, and when illuminated from under the baseboard the resulting 'fire glow' was most convincing.

Next to this, the partially burnt house has glowing embers on the roof, some made with spots of Day-Glo paint and some by leading single optic fibres up to holes drilled in the plaster roof. Although it can't be seen from this angle, the interior of this house also looks suitably ablaze. Fibre optics once again provide the illumination, but in this case I wanted the effect of swirling smoke lit from below by the fire. I first tried using the Christmas tree decoration called 'angel hair', but this had a peculiar property of casting the light in distinct circles and looked unrealistic.

Next I tried some acrylic wadding that my wife uses when making quilts, and this turned out to be ideal; the light from the optics was

diffused throughout the interior of the house and gave me just the effect I wanted. (This material is also used for stuffing soft toy animals and should be available from any good craft shop.)

I would repeat, however, that convincing smoke effects really demand the confinement and control associated with boxed dioramas or building interiors rather than the 'open air'. The effects arrived at in this model do not really show up in this 'natural light' photo - it was the night time lighting in the final display which made all the difference.

To clarify one point, all these 1/62nd scale dioramas made for the museum at Zug had to show just a portion of each village; palisades don't encircle the entire scenes, and houses are sometimes cut through leaving only the end gable and a few feet of wall.

CHAPTER 7
JUNGLE

ABOVE & OPPOSITE Examples of jungle vegetation using photo-etched brass plants. This range of pictures was kindly taken for me by Dominique Breffort of 'Figurines' magazine at the EuroMilitaire show at Folkestone in September 1999. The model is a display by Scale Link Ltd of some of their photo-etched plants, and I'm grateful for their permission to reproduce it here.

Jungles come in many guises and you have a lot of choice when modelling them. You need to refer to reference books and any sources of photos which you can find, in order to establish which kind of jungle grows in the area you are setting out to represent. You can model mountainous or hill terrain, flat or swampy ground, covered with thick or thin jungle, bamboo forest, or even – God help you – elephant grass… .

Primary jungle has massive trees, with the canopy high above the ground; what undergrowth has managed to sprout beneath this canopy is starved of sunlight and thus pretty sparse. It is not nearly as vigorous as that found in secondary jungle, which has masses of thick, tangled undergrowth with everything struggling up towards the light. This is usually the result of either mankind clearing the trees at some point in the past, or some natural catastrophe like a forest fire, which opens up the soil to the sun.

Repeating my remarks in Chapter 4, I believe you should be able to make anything from spindly, open-growth trees to magnificent 'jungle giants' if you follow Barry Bowen's method of tree-building, and these can be further embellished with hanging lianas and creepers. In the vignette I've made for this book the trees are – as in my autumn woodland scene – detailed only 'as far up as you can see', since one point of the model is to show what is going on at ground level. For a full-scale diorama you would be well advised to accept that the finished height will have to be less than an accurate scale representation of the real thing (in primary jungle the canopy can be well over 100 feet high).

There are plenty of good reference photos from the Burma and South-West Pacific campaigns of World War II to give you ideas for your model, as well as the vast library of pictures taken during the Vietnam war, which mostly have the advantage of being in colour.

VIETNAM SWAMP

I must admit that this was the one model that I was most nervous about starting. The effect of somone wading through scummy water was one that I hadn't tried before, and so I put it off until it was the last vignette left to do and I had no choice but to get on with it. All which goes to prove that you don't know what you can do until you try. If there is some new effect which you'd like to use in a diorama but you don't think you can, grasp your courage with both hands, your nose between two fingers, and jump in. You will probably surprise yourself – and there are few better moments . . . .

After planning the layout on my baseboard I laid down the basic groudnwork with Celluclay. I pre-coloured this using a pinky-red powdered poster paint to get that distinctive Vietnam muddy clay look. While this dried I started making some fairly hefty trees. I wanted this to be primary jungle, where the huge trees soar up to the sky and their shadows restrict the growth on the jungle floor. The trees are balsa dowel covered with plaster - not with Flexibark this time, because in most of the photos I've seen of this type of jungle the trees appear to have smoothish bark, and I wanted this 'generic' effect even though I was not trying to model specific species.

Once the plaster was set I made the big 'buttress'-type roots from roughly shaped pieces of balsa wood, with the edges slightly sanded down. I stuck these to the trunks with PVA, and then used plaster to attach the trees to the base. When the trees were set I coloured them with a grey-green wash, and then added some smaller roots made from two–part epoxy putty. From the same material I fashioned some vines which I attached to the tree trunks. For one of the vines, at the back, I cut out large tropical-looking leaves from some very thin foil and stuck them to the vine with PVA.

The next step was to start putting on the tangled growth climbing up the trees. This was done by draping lengths of poly-fibre, with glued-on ground scatter, up and down the trunks, and tacking it here and there with PVA.

Then I began adding the growth on the jungle floor. I've used one or two small pieces of dried plants which I took from my garden, but most of this vegetation is etched brass. With most of the plants in place I started adding a thick leaf litter made with my usual mix of thyme and rosemary leaves, ground up small with my pestle and mortar. These were scattered in and out amongst the trees and plants, and given a final light spray with

OPPOSITE PAGE TOP The trees, covered with plaster and with the balsa 'buttress' roots added.

OPPOSITE CENTRE The painted trees with the smaller roots and vines added from epoxy putty. Note the red earth colour.

OPPOSITE BOTTOM Jungle growth climbing the trees, made from poly-fibre and green ground scatter. Note the leaves on one vine cut from thin metal foil.

THIS PAGE TOP Adding the jungle floor growth around the bases of the trees, using Scale Link etched brass vegetation.

LEFT With the etched brass plants all in place, I added thick layers of leaf scatter across the whole scene.

LEFT A close-up of the completed jungle floor, with the red clay path coming down through the trees. This has been touched in with semi-gloss to achieve a suitably wet, sticky look for the clay.

Letraset Matt varnish. This is an aerosol matt varnish used to seal pencil drawings; it's a very fine spray and sets quite sufficiently to hold light ground scatter in place. I added a fallen branch sticking out from the edge and, drilling a small hole in the baseboard where the swamp water was to be added, I stuck in a piece of root as a floating branch.

When I built the baseboard I had cut three strips of clear plasticard and stuck them to the two sides and the front of the board, to contain the 'water' when I poured it on. Because the swamp water would be opaque I didn't bother to paint any detail on the baseboard, but just in case the colour did show through at any point I laid a single coat of khaki acrylic across the whole thing.

The two wading soldiers are from Verlinden, the second one being slightly modified by the addition of an ammo box on his shoulder. These figures are both modelled to just about chest height and can be stuck straight onto the baseboard after painting. With the figures in place I left the model for about 24 hours, to ensure that everything was dry before I started pouring on the resin 'water'.

Before mixing the resin I used a small spirit level to make sure that the model was sitting level from front to back and side to side. If it had been uneven when I added the resin to it the swamp water, when set, would have had a distinct uphill slope in one direction or another - not very convincing.

My water effect in this case was to be achieved with Micro-Mark 'Ultra-Glo' 50/50 two-part resin. I poured the required amount of resin into a disposable plastic cup and then added a mix of dark brown and olive green 'Vitrail' glass paint, which was then stirred in thoroughly to ensure an even colour. With this done, I added the hardener and, once again, gave the whole thing a good stir. When I could see that the colour was evenly distributed throughout the resin I poured it onto the model. As it poured, I gently tilted the baseboard this way and that to make sure I got the resin as level as I could. Once the water level was up to the soldiers' chests I stopped pouring and left the resin to set, which took about 48 hours.

Before it had set completely hard I scattered some very fine ground cover, to represent algae, over the surface of the resin, deliberately making the coat thicker in one place than another so that the dark water 'grinned' through here and there, giving a nice uneven, blotchy look to the swamp growth. As

I did this I left two patches of water completely clear behind the figures, where they had pushed the growth aside as they waded through the water. If you try this with a stick in a patch of scummy water you'll see the scum closes up again after the stick moves on; so, in the model, the algae has closed in again behind the two soldiers. Once the resin was completely set, I gave the algae a light coat of the Letraset Matt Varnish - not in this case to secure the greenery, since that was stuck to the resin, but to tone down the colour a bit and to make it darker, as though the algae was damp on the surface.

The final touches were the addition of some weed hanging on the floating branch in the foreground, and some leaf scatter fallen from the jungle canopy onto the surface of the swamp. The weed is just a little piece of cotton wool, teased out and coloured with green ink.

OPPOSITE PAGE TOP The two Verlinden GI figures have been stuck to the khaki-painted 'swamp' section of the baseboard with PVA.

OPPOSITE CENTRE The Micro-Mark 'Ultra-Glo' resin, pre-coloured with 'Vitrail' glass paints, has been poured onto the base, confined by the three strips of clear plasticard which had been cemented to the side

and front edges of the board.

OPPOSITE BOTTOM Fine green scatter has been spread across the surface of the resin to represent the scummy algae covering the stagnant water.

THIS PAGE TOP In this shot you can see the areas of clear water behind the two figures. Final touches are floating leaves fallen from the trees overhead,

and the cotton wool weeds hanging on the floating branch in the left foreground.

ABOVE LEFT Coming clean: an uncropped shot showing the true height of the modelled trees. At the planning stage you will have to decide how you are going to display the finished model - whether as a boxed diorama, in a display case with

an obscured 'roof', or in some other way which accomodates the way you choose to handle the problem of scale trees...

ABOVE RIGHT ...But you can have a lot of fun achieving photographic effects by lighting and cropping carefully. This picture is included for no other reason than that it is very moody, and I love it.

MUDDY TRACKS

Really wet mud doesn't hold the definition of tyre treads as well as snow, as it tends to ooze back into the impressions left by the tread. These few shots give you an idea of a wet, sticky track such as you might find in the Pacific theatre. I first covered the baseboard with a nice layer of muddy-coloured Celluclay, and then planted the vegetation along the bank. This is a mixture of a basic layer of ground cover and pieces of a plastic flower display I picked up. I haven't painted it as I think the plastic gives the impression of the shiny, fleshy leaves of tropical plants in the rainy season. Next, I laid on another coat of Celluclay and tried out the position for a Jeep that I'd built some time ago. Removing the model, I fitted a Jeep wheel from the spares box onto a small screwdriver and ran it up and down in the mud to get the churned-up effect that I wanted. (Incidentally, armies fighting in mud often attach snow chains to their vehicle tyres.) Before this layer of Celluclay had set I put the Jeep back in position and left the whole lot to dry out. This done, I muddied the Jeep up with the same coloured Celluclay as the track, applying a fairly thick layer along the edge of the body and under the wheel arches. I then sprayed the track and bottom part of the Jeep with satin finish varnish. A lighter application of FX Mud higher up the body and over the stowage finished off this little tropical scene.

TOP Unlike snow, heavy mud doesn't hold sharp impressions of tyre tracks very well.

CENTRE Temporarily mount a wheel of the same size and tread pattern as those on your model on some handy 'axle', and run it back and forth through the mud.

RIGHT Don't forget that a vehicle such as this will not only collect mud around the bottom of the bodywork, but it will also be very evident where the crew have climbed in and out, on the floor pan, and on any packs strapped to the outside where the wheels throw it up.

LEFT & BELOW 'Cave-Busters', a diorama inspired by an M3 half-track/40mm Bofors conversion which I found attractively dangerous-looking (see also Chapter 2, page 31). Small numbers of these were produced by the US 99th Ordnance Depot at Coopers Plain, Australia, and saw action with the US Army's 299th AAA Bn in ground combat during the liberation of the Philippines in 1944-45. The tactics used were to drive them along one side of a valley and bombard Japanese-held caves and bunkers on the other side. The diorama shows the crew replenishing ammunition and preparing to change barrels. Note the water seepage on the rock face, and the plentiful jungle growth; the clump of bamboo on the outer edge of the track is made from real dwarf bamboo stems from my garden, with added paper leaves.

CHAPTER 8
MORE WATER EFFECTS

As we have already seen in Chapters 2 and 7, you can recreate water in a number of ways, and which medium you choose depends upon what your model represents. For bodies of still water like lakes, ponds and swamps a clear two-part resin is probably the best choice.

It finds its natural level when poured. You can use it 'as it comes' for really clear water, and in such cases you may want to incorporate visible underwater detail work. Alternatively you can tint it before use to create dirty, polluted or stagnant water. If using resin for a fairly deep body of water, don't pour it all on at once; add it in layers, giving each layer time to set before adding the next. If you are tinting it, try adding less and less colour to each layer of resin - this will add to the impression of depth.

Resin sets by a chemical reaction between the resin and the hardener, and heat is generated by this reaction; add too much too quickly, and the surface of the resin tends to craze, ruining the effect. If you want to add ripples to the finished surface, use a hair dryer or heat gun before the resin finally sets, working it across the surface in the direction of the 'wind'.

Another medium for modelling still water is one of the gel products such as Nimix (see Appendix). You melt the gel down and then add it to the model - it takes longer to set than resin but it doesn't need to be mixed with a hardener. The one drawback that I find with this medium is that it stays slightly tacky for a very long time; if you are using it, try to keep your finished model in a display case or cupboard so that dust doesn't collect on the gel surface, destroying the illusion.

If you're making a body of water with a very rough or wind-torn surface, or waves running on to a beach, then painted and varnished plaster is probably easiest. This is described and illustrated in the section on the mountain gorge in Chapter 2, and again with the Normandy and Pacific beach vignettes in Chapter 9; the photos on pages 89 & 90 also show the effect. Pour the plaster onto the model and let it start to set; before it does, lay a piece of clear plastic such as 'cling film' on the surface, and create troughs and peaks in the water by pressing a rounded object - like the back of a spoon, or even the ball of your thumb - into the plaster. Remove the plastic sheet and leave the plaster to set. Using acrylic paints, you can then add your colour, be it stormy grey or green, with white worked in for the foam. You can also add Artist's Gloss Medium to build up the peaks of waves or heavy ripples, and then touch these in with a thin coat of white.

To make puddles in muddy fields and roads I always use Johnson's 'Klear' floor polish and sealer; you just pour a little onto the model, add a touch of acrylic colour such as ochre or umber to give a muddy appearance, and there's your puddle. Again, this takes a while to dry so, as with all water effects, try to ensure that no dust or bits of ground cover get onto the surface until it has completely set. I usually cut up a piece of brown wrapping paper and lay it over the model until I'm sure nothing unwanted can stick to the surface.

A POND WITH BIRCHES

To enable me to have a reasonable depth to this vignette I made the base from a polystyrene ceiling tile stuck to my baseboard. I pencilled in the outline of the pond and dug it out with a hobby knife. Next I mixed up some Celluclay and lined the pond with a good, thick layer and, while this was drying, covered the rest of the base. When adding the Celluclay to the rim of the pond I deliberately formed an overlap, to enable me to hide the meniscus at the edge of the 'water' when it was added (see below). I painted the bottom of the pond with a light tan earth colour, and added a bluey-green area at the centre for an illision of greater depth.

When the paint had dried I laid on several layers of gloss varnish to seal the Celluclay, as the water mix I was going to add would be quite hot and would find any leaks in the base that I might have missed. With the varnish still a bit tacky, I added a very fine layer of green scatter and also some small stones and gravel, and made sure they were firmly stuck to the bottom. The stones and gravel, from my packets of Talus, are actually a very light, pumice-like material - and it hardly gives a convincing impression if, when you have added your water medium, your admiring audience notices that the rocks are floating!

LEFT Using a thick block of polystyrene to give me depth, I carved out the area for the pond and coated it with Celluclay. The rest of the base was then covered with the same medium, and the pond was painted in a pale sandy-green shade. I've built the ground out to overhang the edge of the water to try to prevent the meniscus showing when the 'instant water' is added.

CENTRE LEFT The middle of the bed of the pond has been painted a darker shade of green, for an illusion of greater depth.

BOTTOM LEFT Different textured scatters in various shades of green have been added to the groundwork around the pond. Bullrushes have been stuck in the shallows; these are brush bristles with a small blob of PVA glue drawn out on their tips. When dry the rushes are shaded in green and the tips in dark brown.

BELOW Working on the silver birch trees. A twig from a garden broom has been painted white for about the bottom half, with poly-fibre added, to which I will next stick the foliage.

With everything securely anchored I added the reeds and bullrushes, made with brush bristles; and pushed the holes into the pond bed where the legs of the wooden staging would eventually be set. I coloured in the reeds; and then turned my attention to the area around the pond.

This I covered first with a layer of fine flock and then with another, coarser layer to give my landscape a fairly uncultivated look. The patch of brambles in the corner was made with teased-out rubberised horsehair, which I then sprayed with thin PVA and added bright green new growth, once again using a medium-coarse scatter. The little flowers around the pond are merely small discs of paper, punched out with my Historex Punch & Die set and then painted variously yellow and white. The larger ones by the brambles are the wax ones from the doll's house shop.

Next I set about the young silver birch trees, using twigs from my faithful garden broom. Painted white and with the trunk markings touched in with matt black, they are probably the easiest tree to model - that's why I like them. I sprayed the twigs with Photo-Mount and attached some poly-fibre, which makes an excellent foundation for tree foliage. A second coating of Photo-Mount was added to the poly-fibre and then a layer of medium grade scatter was sprinkled over the tree, followed by another layer of finer scatter in a slightly different shade of green to add depth to the foliage.

I pushed the finished trees into the polystyrene base, and turned my attention to

ABOVE Close-up of the finished birches, with the distinctive markings on the trunks touched in with matt black, and bright green scatter used as spring foliage.

RIGHT With all vegetation and trees in place, and the bass wood landing stage in position, I was now ready to add the final stage - the water. Small stones have been added to the floor of the pond, and firmly stuck down - the last thing you want is for them to rise and 'float' when you add the water medium.

the wooden staging. This is a very simple construction, made from bass wood and stained with Weather-It. It is best to stain the wood before you glue it together if you are using PVA, as Weather-It will act like water and dissolve the glue. A rusty mooring ring was added to the staging, and the whole thing was then set into the pond bed and fixed to the bank with PVA. I didn't use glue to secure the legs of the staging in the pond floor for the same reason - that the melted gel that I was going to use for the water would have dissolved the glue, discolouring the water. I could have used a waterproof glue but, frankly, the staging was perfectly securely fixed to the bank.

Before moving on to prepare the water, I checked that I had finished all the other steps in this model. There is nothing worse than adding water to a scene and then realizing that you have to add some more static grass, dusty gravel, brick rubble or something. No matter how much care you take you'll never manage to avoid some of it sticking to the surface of the water. This doesn't apply if you have made the water from resin or plaster and have left it to thoroughly cure for some days, but the gel which I intended to use here remains tacky for some time.

The water medium I used is called Nimix Artificial Water, from Historex Agents. Unlike some instant water mediums, it requires no mixing. It comes in a plastic jar as a gel with a slight greenish tinge. You place the opened jar into a saucepan of water that comes about half way up it, and bring the water gently to the boil. As the gel heats it melts. Using a pair of tongs, lift the jar out of the pan and pour it into the water area on your model; it spreads out quickly. I then placed the model in a dust-free cupboard for some 24 hours to protect the surface while it dried.

One problem with almost any medium you use to create water is the dreaded meniscus. This is an effect that takes place as the medium dries. Where it touches the edge of the groundwork (and, as in this case, anything which is embedded in it, like the legs of the staging in the pond), it will creep slightly upwards, and set with a rim of 'water' standing higher than the rest.

There is one dangerous way to avoid this. If you have a fairly wide expanse of 'water' and a flattish bank, you can play a heat gun on it and 'smooth' it out with the heat; but take great care - you can also either melt, or set fire to, the rest of the model! In neither this vignette, nor 'The Shell Crater' in Chapter 11, was there enough space for me to try this.

One answer is to plan for this problem by undercutting your bank from the start, and adding a final layer of groundwork overlapping above this 'ridge' of water, hiding it under some bushes or grass; but do wait until the water is completely dry before you do this (see above). As far as the legs of my staging were concerned, I just had to live with the meniscus.

LEFT The Nimix Artificial Water gel has been poured in and left to set, as described in the body text.

THE CANAL

My purpose in this scene was to try to create a body of water completely covered with a toxic-green scum of algae; so I decided to attempt a canal, with a section of bank and towpath. I have left it without figures for the photos but, of course, canals frequently offered obstacles to the advance of armies in Europe, and this setting would suit a military vignette from 1870, 1914, 1940 or 1944, to mention only the most obvious campaigns. For non-military subjects it would also form a pleasant stage for any number of single figures, strolling couples, small groups of picnickers, etc., with or without fishing kit, dogs, or prams. Or how about a Sunday painter with stool and easel?

I made the base from MDF (see page 19) and marked out my areas as usual, to give an idea of proportion. You don't have to make the canal section as deep as I did - it's just the way it came out.

The first job was building the retaining wall of brick sets. I used a fairly stout piece of cardboard for this, as I didn't want it warping when I covered it with glue. I marked out the spacing for the sets, leaving gaps for the mortar, and fitted a small piece of plastic tubing as the mouth of a drain. I made the brick sets themselves by casting them in plaster which had been pre-coloured red/brown with powdered poster paint, using a silicone mould (see Chapter 11, in the section on the 'Shell Crater'). You could equally make them out of thin card or heavy paper.

I glued cardboard formers in place to support my towpath, and then glued the retaining wall into place against them. Next, I added a line of fine green ground cover along the high water mark on the wall, and also one

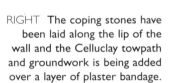

ABOVE The brick sets laid out on the cardboard backing. Although cast in pre-coloured plaster, these need some touching up with paint afterwards to vary their exact shades.

RIGHT The brick retaining wall attached to the formers which provide a frame for the towpath. The wall is already sprouting some vegetation.

RIGHT The coping stones have been laid along the lip of the wall and the Celluclay towpath and groundwork is being added over a layer of plaster bandage.

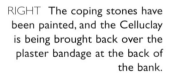

RIGHT The coping stones have been painted, and the Celluclay is being brought back over the plaster bandage at the back of the bank.

RIGHT The bank has been scattered with ground cover and the flowers added. I've made two large mooring posts from pieces of driftwood; these are black below the waterline, green with growth at water level, and natural weather-faded colour above. Note the rusty iron rings and mooring chains. Nothing remains to be done but to pour on the plaster 'water'.

or two etched brass plants. At the same time I pushed etched brass ferns right into a couple of the mortar courses of the wall, together with an occasional clump of dark green 'weeds'.

The formers for the towpath were covered with masking tape and then with a layer of plaster bandage. On this I spread a layer of Celluclay, pre-coloured with a light soil-coloured acrylic paint. The coping stones, stuck along the edge of the path with PVA glue, were cast in plaster from a rubber mould which came from a building kit called 'Castle Master'. I picked this up years ago and I doubt you will be able to find it in the shops now, but it is worth keeping your eyes open at boot fairs, etc., because it has some very useful moulds for casting stones, stone window arches, pillars and many other 'castle' bits that come in handy in a diorama. Once in place the stones were coloured with an acrylic stone-grey paint and highlighted with a paler grey.

The towpath was then gravelled using Woodland Scenics' fine grade Talus; and I glued in the line of growth along the inside of the coping stones. The larger plants on that side of the path are from Scale Link's range of etched brass flowers and riverside plants. Having painted the bank beside the path in a shade of light tan earth colour, I spread a layer of thin PVA and covered it with a random scattering of fine ground cover, deliberately leaving one or two patches of the earth showing through since this is not meant to be a well-kept, cultivated piece of land. Next I glued coarse ground cover onto the bank as rough, weedy growth, and then added the yellow flowers. Once again, these are the wax jobs which come from a shop selling supplies for makers of doll's houses.

The weathered timbers are bits of driftwood from the beach. I painted them with an almost black-green at the bottom, and then added a ring of bright green algae at the high water mark. Small bits of chain were threaded through a couple of 'iron rings', which came from an old necklace. The rust effect is created with shades of orange, brown and black paint, with a little orange pastel chalk dust mixed in for texture.

It was now time to add the 'water'. In this case, as it was to be totally opaque, I mixed up some plaster and added powdered green poster paint until I had a lovely poisonous green. (You have to juggle the quantities until you get the shade you want when adding paint to plaster; the whiteness of the plaster knocks back the colour of your paint quite

considerably.) Once I was happy with the colour I poured the plaster into the scene and left it to set. The very slightly textured effect of the algae on the water was achieved by making no effort to get all the air bubbles out of the plaster before it set. Once it had done so, I next thickened up the line of growth along the water line, made from ground cover and some paper reeds; and added a bit more algae to the rusty chains.

With the planting done, I painted in a line of open water along the weed margin. Deep, dirty water with no light getting to it looks almost totally black; I touched this area in with black Indian ink, so as to have a slightly shiny finish. Finally, I watered the ink right down and used it to create the staining under the mouth of the drain in the canal wall.

TOP & ABOVE The plaster 'water' has been poured in, and the weeds along the foot of the wall have been added from a mixture of ground cover and a few etched brass leaves. The texture of the algae-covered surface is provided by the plaster itself - I deliberately didn't remove the air bubbles. The line of glossy black water at the edge is painted with Indian ink.

TOP A shot of the finished canal vignette. Note the algae growing up the posts; and the knocks and scrapes the brickwork has suffered over the years from passing barges.

ABOVE While making the 1/62nd scale dioramas for the Cantonal Early History Museum at Zug, Switzerland, I tried using two different water mediums. In this overhead view of part of a Neolithic lakeside village (c5000-2200 BC) the water is Nimix gel, with the stones and weeds stuck to the lake bottom before pouring it on. The reeds are painted brush bristles.

LEFT In the Bronze Age village diorama (c2200-800 BC), also illustrated in Chapter 6, the lake had to be wind-ruffled to support the impression of stormy weather. I used plaster, pushing the waves in with my finger tips through a temporary cover of cling-film. Once dry, I painted it a murky green with a touch of sand colour to re-create the effect of the bottom being stirred up. The wave tops were built up with Artist's Gloss Medium touched in with white acrylics.

BELOW The real thing. Fast streams always carry debris, which gets hung up on the banks lower down - usually at the outside of bends, as well as on rocks or other obstructions.

RIGHT The real thing. Notice the transparency of this clear mountain stream. The rocky bed shows different colours: in a model they would have to be painted in carefully before adding any poured water medium.

RIGHT The real thing. Dead leaves floating on only an inch or two of water will cast shadows. The textures of the puddle floor show clearly.

ABOVE & RIGHT The early medieval village diorama for the museum at Zug (also illustrated in Chapter 5) had to feature a river rushing past in autumn spate, dirty with stirred-up silt. I made this, too, of painted plaster with a layer of Artist's Gloss Medium laid on top. This was left for about 20 to 30 minutes to semi-set before the ripples were pushed into its surface.

CHAPTER 9
SAND & GRAVEL

It seems logical to discuss beach and desert effects together, since modelling both may demand, to some extent, the same sort of materials.

Sand and gravel are usually to be found in models of warfare in the North African desert or the Pacific. Beach sand needs to be as fine as you can find; obviously, to scale down what is already a fine, powdery material in real life to 1/35th scale is almost impossible, so once again we allow some artistic licence. Some of the sands you can find in pet shops for spreading in the bottom of birdcages can be pretty fine. The Western Desert of Egypt and the coastal strip of Libya where much of the fighting took place is more often stony than sandy. Obviously, if you're modelling the great sand dunes of the true Sahara or Arabia then you are back to a fine material. For the more stony type of desert there is a very simple material available – cat litter.

Most cat litters are made from absorbent products such as granulated atapulgite, which will absorb acrylic colours as readily as they do less pleasant things. You can crush the material up very easily and create as coarse or as fine a gravel as you want. You can also buy railway modellers' Gravel Matting, such as that made by Gaugemaster (see Appendix), if you need the basis for covering a large area.

OMAHA BEACH

My 'Omaha Beach' vignette is intended to show you how to create the effect of wet, rippled sand, and the way ebbing water scours depressions at the foot of anything set on the beach.

The base is a bit of MDF covered with a thin layer of plaster which I mixed up with sand-coloured water. I smoothed this out across the base with an artist's palette knife, and while it was still damp I used a small, flat-bladed dental tool to carve very shallow wavy lines along the length of the sand. At the same time I made the indentations where the beach defences would stand. These are an old Tamiya product; I had made them up before laying out my beach, so as to be able to measure the correct distance between the feet.

When the 'sand' had set I built up the shingle at the back; I had used the usual strip of polystyrene to embank this area. The shingle itself is a strange mixture of Talus, various spice seeds and sago. This tasty mix was sprinkled on to a thick layer of PVA, and further layers were added until I had the depth of shingle I wanted. I secured it with a final spraying of Scenic Cement.

Next I set the rusty beach defences in place in their indentations in the sand. If you have noticed, as the water flows off a beach it scoops out a depression at the base of any rock, post, pipe or any other projection; this is caused by the swirling motion of the water as it flows around the obstruction, taking the sand away. When my beach defences were in place, the prepared 'dimples' gave just this effect. The ironwork was then treated to a dressing of barnacles and other small bits of detritus. This included tiny shreds of seaweed, made from very small pieces of a dried moss – I would also add this for the seaweed left washed up on the beach. All of this was then coated in gloss varnish. I also filled the depressions in the

ABOVE The basic sandy-coloured plaster has been laid and the shingle bank added. In this picture the ripples carved in the sand are not too distinct, but the scooped-out hollows where the second beach defence will be placed are quite clear. I have laid the first layer of very thin plaster for the foam, and washed the beach over with a layer of gloss varnish.

ABOVE LEFT With the rusty beach defence in place I have added various marine encrustations, and strands of seaweed made from a very fine moss. When the glue holding this in place had dried I coated it with two or three layers of gloss varnish, which not only gave it a wet look but helped make it hang down.

sand with several coats of gloss varnish, and coated the whole beach again, to give a shiny, wet finish to the sand.

Next came the sea, which is a further layer of plaster laid on with a slightly uneven surface. When dry this was painted with shades of green acrylic, with white streaks worked into the green to look like foam just below the surface; and finished with several coats of gloss varnish. The white foamy edge of the ripples was formed by spreading a very thin layer of plaster into which, once it had almost dried, I worked the bristle end of a small paintbrush, stippling it like a stencil brush. This revealed areas of the sandy colour underneath, and created the ragged, lacy look of thin foam. I built up the foam in odd places by adding a little more plaster on top, particularly where it is draining out over the abandoned M1 carbine. Finally I painted all the foam matt white, with just a touch of gloss here and there to sparkle in the light.

ABOVE Both tripods are in place, and the plaster 'sea' has been painted with acrylics. When this has dried you will need to patiently add several layers of gloss varnish to get a really wet look - the plaster tends to absorb the first coats.

RIGHT A view of the finished model with the last thin layer of foam added; the streaks of white paint help give the impression of the water draining back from the beach. A scattering of seaweed has been added along the shingle bank and in random strands over the whole beach.

RIGHT Viewed from the 'landward' side of the scene, you can see the build-up of the foam where it is running back over the abandoned M1 carbine. The wet ripples in the sand show up quite well here, too.

SOUTH PACIFIC

By contrast with the chilly glisten of Normandy's wet sand and shingle, this next vignette is a very simple demonstration of a Pacific seashore. The basic method is adaptable for any suitable scene, from a boatload of 17th century pirates landing to bury treasure to the US Marines hitting the beach at Tarawa.

As usual, I started out by gluing a strip of polystyrene to give myself a raised area of land at the rear of the beach. (I have tended to do this with most of the vignettes in this book; I think the raised embankment at the back of a scene makes a neat visual 'finishing point' for the model.) This was then covered with plaster bandage and, when it was dry, I added a layer of plaster to form the beach itself, feathering this into the plaster bandage so that there was no rigid demarcation line between the two areas.

The next move was adding the sand. It is quite difficult to find a medium that will give you convincing scale sand, but I settled for a grade which I believe is fine enough to look the part. This came from a car repair shop and was used in a sand-blasting cabinet for cleaning down panels to base metal prior to undercoating. To get the sand to stick, I

ABOVE I've covered the polystyrene base with sand on the beach, and the dune area with plaster bandage, also painted in a sandy shade.

ABOVE A second layer of sand has been added to the beach, and footprints have been impressed into it with the blunt end of a paintbrush, using a backwards and forwards rocking motion. The whole area was then sprayed with Scenic Cement to hold everything in place. The plaster sea has been added, with the small wavelets sculpted into it before the plaster had dried out completely. It was then painted and varnished.

LEFT Sparse and scrubby vegetation is added to the top of the beach. This is a fairly coarse scatter with mixed shades of green.

RIGHT The basis for the palm trees was two short lengths of old multi-core cable.

BELOW They were first wound with wire, then coated in plaster.

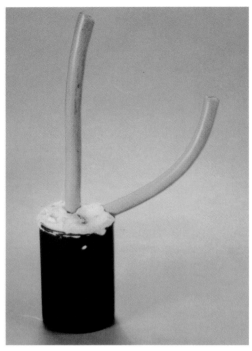

ABOVE With a crown added from 'thatch' material, they were painted in a pale grey-green shade, the growth rings picked out by shading the underside of the 'lumps' with a darkish brown.

RIGHT The beach with a washed-up and partly buried palm log added. The sea was painted with a deep greeny-blue to simulate the deeper water; the same shade was used with the addition of increasing amounts of matt white to show it getting progressively shallower. When I reached the forward edges of the waves and the final line of foam on the beach I used almost pure white. Several coats of gloss varnish were added when the paint was dry.

flooded both the plaster of the beach and the plaster bandage with Woodland Scenics thin PVA glue, and scattered a liberal coating on from my flour shaker, leaving a bare strip at the front of the base where I was going to put in the waves. I left this to dry and, after shaking off the excess, repeated the operation, gradually building up a layer thick enough to enable me to mark in footprints.

I added these at this stage, at the same time placing the washed-up piece of palm trunk. The footprints were made by pushing the

rounded end of a paint brush into the sand and rocking it backwards and forwards. The washed-up trunk is plaster, cast from an old one which I had in stock, using latex to create the mould. When this had all dried I shook off the excess sand again, and gave the whole area a coating of hair spray to hold everything in place.

The edge of the sea was made from another layer of plaster, treated exactly as on 'Omaha Beach' above. This was laid on fairly thick and then the waves were sculpted in while it was still damp. When I was happy with the shape, I painted the water using acrylic paints. Into the base coat of greeny-blue I blended streaks of white for the combers and the foam. Blend this in while the base coat is still wet and you get a good effect of depth. I finished painting by touching in the very front edge of some of the combers and the foam on the beach with undiluted pure white paint. When the sea had dried I painted on a coat of high gloss varnish and, once dry, another, and so on until I had built up about six layers of varnish to give a really 'wet' look as well as adding to the impression of depth.

Going back to the edge of the 'dunes', I sprayed the groundwork with thin PVA and added some ground cover. I sprinkled this on quite thinly to get the effect of the sparse growth often found at the top of beaches.

Next came the palm trees. I made these in a way similar in some respects to the method used by Barry Bowen (see Chapter 4), but perhaps a bit quicker. Firstly I took a couple of

lengths of multi-core cable and bent them to the rough shape I wanted for the finished tree. Next I bound the trunks with wire, working from the base up. I worked first from right to left around the trunk, and then from left to right, so that I finished up with the wires crossing over one another and giving the 'bumpy' look I needed. I then covered the trunks in ready-mixed Fine Crack Filler paste. You can get this from any DIY shop – Polyfilla do one, but there are several other makes. I finished off by building up a slightly bulbous head to each trunk.

Using some material which I bought in a doll's-house supply shop, which was being sold as thatch, I built up a 'crown' around the top of the trees and a 'collar' around the base. I then painted the trunks, using a mixture of pale tan and green, with the 'bumps' picked out in a darker brown. When the paint was dry I added the palm fronds which, in this case, were from the Scale Link range of etched brass foliage.

(By the way, as you can see, I used my favourite method of mounting practically anything I am working on which requires to be held – the Mk I Plasticine-filled Empty 35mm Film Canister. Any camera shop will let you have some of these free of charge; they're usually only too glad to get rid of them. Just fill them with plasticine and stick in your work piece – a tree, a figure, weapons, whatever. It allows you to roll the canister between your fingers to get at any part of the item for painting without touching it. Not very sophisticated, but much cheaper than buying an expensive clamp, and just as efficient.)

ABOVE & LEFT Final views of the finished vignette. The palm trees have been installed and their etched-brass fronds added. A helmet lies abandoned above a scattering of seashells at the water's edge – these are tiny pieces of Woodland Scenics pummice-like Talus.

RIGHT 'Welcome Aboard!' - the commander of an M4A1 Sherman of the US 10th Army offers a sailor a tour of his tank during the Pacific campaign. The beach is basically Celluclay with a top covering of fine sand, held in place with a spray of Scenic Cement.

RIGHT Two of the tank crew work on an engine problem. The vegetation on the right is from a florist's shop.

RIGHT The palm trees are made from plaster-covered wire, and the leaves are cut from the soft metal of a drinks can. The vegetation at the base of the palms is ground scatter, and the grasses are Woodland Scenics 'Field Grass'.

NORTH AFRICAN TRACK

Most of the battlefields fought over during the epic Western Desert campaigns between British 8th Army and Rommel's Deutsches Afrikakorps looked nothing whatever like the rolling sand dunes of 'Lawrence of Arabia'. The surface was sand, of course, but it was very stony, thickly scattered with mostly light-coloured rocks and gravel of every size. In many places sheets of bedrock were only a couple of feet below the surface, making 'digging in' almost impossible. In some areas there was a randomly spaced-out growth of low weeds and camel-thorn. The very simple vignette shown here represents a small section of this type of terrain, combined with a vehicle track; using the same materials it could be extended convincingly to a full-size diorama.

First, I stuck my usual small strip of polystyrene to the rear edge of the baseboard to give a raised feature next to the track. I then covered the base and polystyrene with a layer of Celluclay, tinted with an acrylic Dark Sand paint. While this coat was still damp, I used a kit wheel from the spares box to make tyre tracks in the sand, varying the angle of the tracks as trucks would not be following exactly the same line.

I then air-brushed random areas of the groundwork with a very thin wash of a slightly lighter shade of sand to give variety to the overall colour. As soon as this was done I alsopushed 'stones' of varying size into the soft clay - once again, from Woodland Scenics Talus. As well as coming in packets of coarse, medium and fine grades, this is usefully supplied in two colours, natural and brown, and both accept acrylic paints; I stuck it to the groundwork with white PVA. I then put everything to one side to dry.

Once the groundwork had dried, I applied areas of Woodland Scenics' thin PVA glue and scattered green flock in random patches to represent low, weedy growths. The last pieces of vegetation to be added were one or two clumps of camel-thorn. For this I used lichen, both in a green shade and also in a bleached-out colour to represent dead bushes, and again secured these with white PVA.

To add a little interest I made up a unit road sign. Where the rock was too close to the surface for trail-markers to stick a signpost in the ground, they often used old fuel drums filled with stones to make a secure base. My 45-gallon drum is from the old Tamyia Drum & Jerrycan set. I painted the red and white segments on the barrel and, when dry, worked it over with rust-coloured streaks and scrapes, again varying the colour. (Yes, things do rust during the desert nights.) I didn't fit the top, but filled it instead with sand-coloured Celluclay; then I pushed in the hand-painted sign and, while the clay was still damp, added the large 'stones' that wedge the sign in place.

ABOVE The remains of the fire, made by the crew from a broken-up wooden cargo palette and a C-ration carton to burn their trash; you can just see where it has scorched some of the vegetation. Other rubbish is tossed into the oil drum - rags, an empty oil can, and so on. The length of rusty Pierced Steel Plate 'sand matting' is from my spares box. Verlinden and other firms make PSP in resin or metal - the latter is obviously more realistic.

RIGHT The basic layout for the North African track. The base-board is covered firstly with sand-coloured Celluclay, and then sprayed with adhesive to secure layers of sprinkled sand. Before it dries the tyre tracks are pressed in and the spot where the oil drum will go is marked.

RIGHT The next step is adding the stones and gravel, from ground-up Talus.

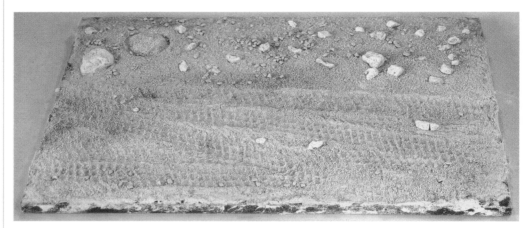

RIGHT Small areas are spotted with glue, and fine ground cover is then sprinkled in a random fashion to simulate low, scrubby growth.

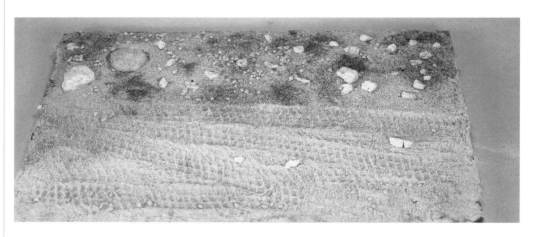

RIGHT Clumps of camel-thorn are added, made from lichen (frankly, I believe this is about the only thing the stuff is useful for).

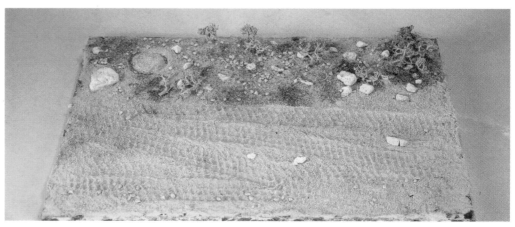

LEFT & ABOVE The final touch: the unit track marker sign, wedged in its drum full of stones, is glued into place.

BELOW A shot of a partially finished diorama of a ruined Roman building in Tunisia. All parts for the ruin were cast in plaster using the moulds of the old 'Castle Master' kit described in Chapter 8. The prickly pears in the background are made from Milliput. The gravelly sand is ground-up cat litter stuck to a plaster base with PVA.

CHAPTER 10
TRACKS & ROADS

OPPOSITE PAGE TOP Static grass runs down the central strip of our muddy lane, and the puddles have been filled with Johnson's 'Klear' tinted ochre.

Roads appear in a great number of dioramas, whatever the subject or period of history. Dirt roads and tracks lend themselves to very effective representations of the seasons - hard, rutted, bone-white, dusty roads in the summer; churned-up, wet, muddy tracks with deep puddles in the autumn; frozen ruts, slush and puddles skinned with 'cat ice' in the winter.

To ring the changes, it can be fun to build a corduroy road. From prehistoric times to World War II in Russia this crude but effective form of reinforcing dirt surfaces was used to help transport men, horses, carts and trucks over muddy ground. It ranged from carefully cut, trimmed and laid tree trunks, to simply piling branches, saplings or thick piles of brush to provide traction. Only recently, such a prehistoric track system was found in one of the swampier areas of Britain. It consisted of layers of brushwood laid crosswise, edged with saplings laid across the ends parallel to the track and pinned down with forked twigs to hold the whole thing in place. In model form this is very simply done by using twigs of varying thickness, laid into a bed of suitably coloured Celluclay. Dirty the end result with mud or, for a winter scene, powder it with

dirty snow and border it with slush.

Muddy tracks or lanes are best made with Celluclay. Puddles can be made by making indentations in your mud and then, when dry, pouring in small amounts of gloss varnish or Johnson's 'Klear' liquid floor polish. For small frozen puddles, paint the bottom of the puddle in a shade of dark grey and drip candle wax into the depression. The wax tends to mound in the centre as it sets, so when it is fully set hold a hot iron just above the wax, and it will melt again and flow out flat. (But don't touch the wax with the iron - not if you don't want to be ironing your own shirts for the next six months.)

Ditches can be cut into a polystyrene baseboard and lined with Celluclay. If it is a dry ditch, add a growth of weeds and flowers, both in the bottom and on the lip. A damp ditch can be represented by just coating the bottom with satin varnish and small amounts of green ground cover to represent algae. To model a very wet ditch, coat the bottom with several layers of gloss varnish with, perhaps, a couple of small branches made from twigs lying in the bottom. For one that is actually running with water, use one of the methods described in this book for modelling water, again adding weeds

RIGHT The shape of the lane has been laid out using pieces of polystyrene glued to the base-board, and the overall layer of Celluclay has dried. I've started adding the ruts on the trackway and making the slight depressions for the puddles.

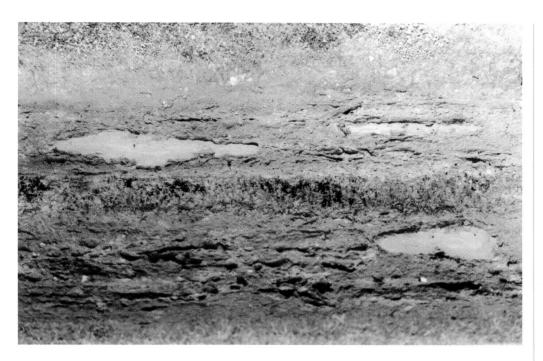

and reeds to the bottom and banks. Grassy banks tend to be greener further back from the track or road; the growth by the edge of the road is often dead and appears as a tan or pale straw colour. Before the mid - 20th century the grass along roadsides and tracks would be mixed with flowering weeds, like the arable fields and meadows.

If you're making a road or pavement surface from plaster and you're engraving kerbstones and/or a pattern of flag stones rather than making individual stones, then give the plaster some texture by pressing a piece of fairly coarse sandpaper into it before it dries. If you don't want to go to the bother of making old flag stones from plaster, a quicker way is to cut them out from cardboard, stick them down, and then paint them stone grey with touches of brown or olive green mixed in. Use a fairly thick piece of card to give the flagstones some depth. Don't forget that unlike modern paving slabs, flags were natural stone and didn't have nicely squared or rectangular shapes, so cut uneven edges. If you intend to put any sort of filling - plaster or Celluclay - between them, give them a coat of varnish first to prevent the water in the grouting mix warping them.

I have given examples in this and the next chapter of how I model dirt roads and those set with cobbles, Roman flags, 17th - 19th century granite sets and poured surfaces such as asphalt and tar macadam. Backgrounds for models of most periods can be adapted from these basic methods. The most timeless (and useful) of all is your basic muddy track.

A MUDDY LANE

The first steps for this vignette were the standard ones already described many times. Strips of polystyrene were glued to the baseboard to create the basic shape of the banks, and a quantity of pre-coloured Celluclay was mixed up. The whole scene was coated with the Celluclay and, when dry, given an overall coat of acrylic earth colour. Next, I created the shallow hollows for the puddles, raising very slight lips around them with Celluclay and putting in the ruts in the 'mud' at the same time. I then added a small amount of yellow ochre acrylic paint to some Johnson's 'Klear' liquid floor wax to make 'muddy water' for my puddles. 'Klear' takes a while to set, so I started making my hollow tree.

The basis of the tree is a length of balsa dowel of 19mm diameter and about 110mm long. I hollowed this out with a ball-headed steel cutter in a Dremel motor drill. The fibrous nature of balsa gives a very natural torn and tatty look to the interior of the trunk. I used the same cutter to make the hollow in the side of the tree, and then added the roots and the burr around the hollow from Duro. When the putty had set I coated the whole tree with Flexibark. This rough-textured paste dries quite quickly.

The inside of the trunk was painted with acrylic dark brown, with a light dry-brushing of lighter brown over some of the roughly splintered wood. The outside was coloured with an earth base coat paint from Woodland Scenics. I then added the ivy tendrils, made from Spanish moss bought from a florist's

RIGHT A view from the back of the tree after painting, which emphasises the texture of Flexibark. The ivy stems have now been added.

FAR RIGHT The ivy is made from Spanish moss and silver birch catkin seeds, all stuck on with PVA glue.

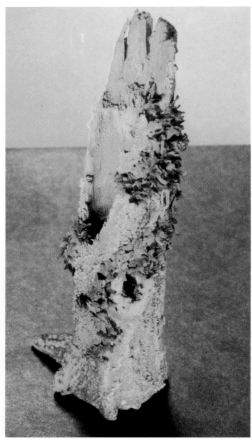

RIGHT The finished tree glued in place.

shop. Next came the slowest part of the job – sticking on the ivy leaves. I'm afraid there is no quick way of doing this; any time you want to create a realistic effect of leaf cover, be it on a wall, a tree or a fence, I'm afraid it's got to be the 'one at a time' method. The ivy leaves were made from silver birch catkin seeds and fixed with PVA glue. When set, I painted them using two or three different shades of green to get contrast in the growth, and used yellow and light brown to add some dead leaves to the picture.

Returning to the lane, it was time to add the ground cover. For the bank in the foreground I merely added some static grass. For the far side I first scattered static grass and then began to build up a more overgrown bank. I used rubberised horsehair for the bramble bushes, and when they were dry added leaves made with tiny pieces of cork and some catkin seeds. I worked the hollow tree's base into some wet Celluclay and blended it all in with the ground. I dry-brushed some very pale tan over the grass to give it an autumnal look, and added the dead bracken by the tree from a pack of brass-etched ferns from Scale Link. You can get them in a variety of sizes, and I think they add a wonderfully realistic touch to almost any groundwork. I used a rusty acrylic colour to paint them, but first I always spray brass-etched formings with an undercoat, usually a neutral grey colour from a car accessory shop. The addition of a dead twig to represent the winter skeleton of a young tree, and a clump of longer dead grass at the side of the track, finished the bank.

The central, untrodden strip of the lane was covered firstly with static grass and some Woodland Scenics scatter, and then I put in some taller dead grass at odd intervals. To complete the vignette I gave the two strips of mud another coating of gloss varnish and, while this was still tacky, I scattered on some more small leaves. I must confess that – seen through the camera viewfinder against sky paper – the final result gave me a good deal of satisfaction.

ABOVE The muddy lane completed. The rough scrub on the far bank is made from rubberised horsehair with leaves from catkin seeds and granualted cork. Photo-etched brass ferns grow at the base of the hollow tree, painted a rusty shade for autumn colouring. Clumps of dead grass have been added and wind-blown leaves have been scattered all over the scene. A final coating of gloss varnish has been applied for a suitably wet look.

LEFT 15th century travellers meet on the lane outside their village. This setting would suit figures from just about any period of European history, and many North American subjects. (The figures were kindly painted by Charles Davis.)

TOP The kerbstones laid out either side of the street and the stepping stones in place. The water trough will fit in the slight gap in the far kerb. I've also added the base of the wider of the two pavements, using a strip of the usual polystyrene tile.

CENTRE The paving stones for the roadway being laid in a bed of earth-coloured Celluclay; the water trough is in place. I've started painting the stones at this point, using a colour mix of earth and grey stone acrylics.

BOTTOM The road stones are all in place and grouted, and I've just filed the two grooves to represent the wear of cart wheels.

A ROMAN STREET

A Roman subject was an obvious choice for a chapter on modelling roads; but for a change I decided to come in out of the countryside and try my hand at an urban vignette. All the main reference for this model came from Peter Connolly's wonderful book *Pompeii* (Macdonald Educational, 1979: ISBN 0 356 06303 8). If you have any interest in building models of this period you could not get a better source of illustrated information.

To recreate this Roman street I began by casting a number of kerbstones and three stepping stones from plaster. I then laid the kerbstones out to give me the width of my street, and put the stepping stones in place; in real life these had to be far enough apart to allow the passage of carts and wagons, but close enough for pedestrians to use them.

Mixing some Celluclay, I next laid down the foundation of the two pavements, leaving a gap for the water trough. The trough came next, cast from some shapes in my 'Castle Master' kit, with the spout made from a short piece of 30 amp fuse wire. Once all this stonework was set I used acrylic stone grey paint with a touch of earth brown to colour the kerbs and the trough, and left it all to dry while I made the stone slabs for the roadway.

These were very simply made by casting a thin slab of plaster and then breaking it up into irregular shapes, rather like crazy paving. Before sticking them down with PVA I gently rounded all the edges off with a file, to give the slabs a used and worn look. Once stuck down on the roadway I grouted them with some more Celluclay. When the glue had dried I used a rounded file to mark in the two grooves worn by the passage of carts. Using a slightly warmer shade of the stone colour I then painted the whole roadway, laying in a darker, earthy wash to emphasize the gaps between the stones and the wheel ruts.

The next step was to make the pavements (sidewalks); and to start with I made a complete mess of this job. The Romans made their pavements by mixing cement and adding in broken-up tiles and bits of brick, so it ended up with a speckled finish. I thought this was simplicity itself – just mix some terra cotta-coloured plaster, let it set, break it up, and then mix the bits in with some plain plaster. But no … As soon as I started adding my bits of broken 'tile' to the plain plaster, the colour seeped out and I wound up with a completely terra-cotta-coloured pavement. Having exhausted my range of basic Anglo-Saxon (which is quite extensive) I gave it some more thought. I finally .came up the answer and, in the process, made the most authentic Roman pavement ever modelled.

I live quite near Canterbury, which was originally a Roman city. Some while ago roadworks were being carried out there and archaeologists came across the foundations of a Roman gatehouse in the city wall. One of them was kind enough to give me a Roman brick from the excavations, which I had put on a shelf and forgotten. Yes, you've guessed it: the pavements in this model are made from a mixture of plaster and fragments of original Roman brick!

Since this was a city scene the model clearly had to be 'finished off' at the back with a section of the wall of a simple Roman shop (closed for business, however - intriguing as it would have been to model part of the interior). The wall is a piece of foam board coated with a thin layer of plaster, which was just deep enough for me to give the impression of the rubble-filled wall underneath where the plaster had cracked. The colours are copied from a building unearthed in Pompeii and, like the simple wooden doors, are based on Peter Connolly's paintings.

Although this was supposed to be an exercise in groundwork, having got this far I couldn't resist finishing touches such as the typical graffiti. Excavations at Pompeii and Herculaneum show that graffiti were very common in 1st century Roman towns; but they were not scratched in standard 'monumental' Latin capitals, and I didn't want to simply invent mine. Luckily a little research turned up some examples, in the characteristic demotic script, in a book called *Herculaneum* by Joseph Jay Deiss (Harper & Row, NY, 1985; ISBN 0 06 015376 8). The upper one beside the shop doorway is an advert for food being sold inside - roughly, 'Pizzas for four pennies'. The female profile - tidied up a little from the original - is accompanied by the sentiment 'Julia, queen of my heart'. (Many of the graffiti found in the buried towns on the bay of Naples extolled the virtues of, shall we say, ladies of negotiable affections. For the record, the most popular girl in town was named Primigenia.)

The final touches to this model were the addition of water in the trough, the broken water jar in the gutter, a few sprouting weeds and the 'horse apples' in the street. The water was made with clear casting resin,

LEFT The water trough is made from plaster cast in a mould meant for making stones for a castle.
The fountain is simply made from square bits of plaster with an old plastic disc on the front and a short piece of fusewire for the spout.

mixed 50/50 resin and hardener, poured and left to set overnight. The water jar was cast in pre-coloured plaster from a silicone mould which I had made for some of the dioramas I built for the museum at Zug, Switzerland. The weeds are simply bristles from a soft brush, stuck between the stones with PVA; and the horse apples are suitably coloured pieces of Celluclay.

ABOVE At left, one of the pavements laid, using crushed (Roman) brick in plaster. (This speckled finish seems to have been quite common in Roman cement, and even in some wall plaster.) The wheel grooves have now been painted in.

RIGHT The Roman shop front, with its battered plastered finish decorated with graffiti.

RIGHT The finished model, complete with the broken water pot and the 'horse apples'. These last must have been an almost universal sight on every kind of track and road, throughout history up until about the 1920s. The scene positively cries out for the figures of a couple of off-duty soldiers heading down town . . . (Incidentally, the only absolutely confirmed skeleton of a Roman soldier ever found was excavated in a street at Herculaneum, killed outright by the blast from Vesuvius. He was not in armour, but was wearing his decorated sword and dagger belts, carrying a tool bag on his shoulders, and had gold and silver coins in his purse.)

A NAPOLEONIC ROAD

This model of a stretch of highroad, based upon a contemporary painting of the Charleroi-Brussels road in the vicinity of Waterloo, was not complicated to make but took a fair amount of patience. (My reference came largely from one of a marvellous new series of books on aspects of Waterloo by Bernard Coppens & Patrice Courcelle, published in Belgium - see Appendix.)

Most European paved roads of this period - mostly dating from the 17th century - were surfaced with granite sets, laid across the width of the road rather than parallel to it, and had a pronounced camber running from the centre to either side. To achieve this I firstly glued a strip of dowel down the centre of the baseboard, and then laid a sheet of thin cardboard over this as the basis for the roadway. A length of polystyrene was stuck along the back and then coated with plaster bandage to make the bank. Once the bandage had set I overlaid it with Celluclay and sprayed on a thin, sandy-coloured wash.

Now I had to build the road surface itself, and there was no quick way of doing this. Using a silicone mould, I cast some 1,000 separate granite sets from a material called Granitex. This is a stone-coloured modelling compound from the same company that make the Sculpey compound, but it has tiny flecks of black in it, giving it a granite look. Once moulded to shape you put it into an oven at 135 degrees C (275 F) for about 15 minutes per quarter-inch of thickness. Obviously my sets were nowhere near that thick, and 'cooked' much quicker. Making the sets did not take too long, but then came the job of laying them, and this did take patience.

I stuck them down onto the cardboard base with PVA, a row at a time, working across the roadbed until the whole road was covered. I realize that a quicker way of doing this would be to take a moulding of a few rows of sets and cast a whole section at a time. My objection to this is that you will end up with a repeating pattern of stones - my way, each one is visibly different.

The width of these roads varied considerably, and the width of one road varied at different points. Contemporary descriptions might list a width of, say, 13 metres (42 feet), but this measurement seems to have been taken between the fronts of buildings on either side and did not indicate the usable width. The paved carriageway was supposed to be wide enough to allow at least

two wagons to pass, but often it was only wide enough for one (e.g. the Charleroi-Brussels road in the Forest of Soignes). Consequently, even in civilian use, most roads had broad strips of beaten-down earth on each side where traffic had been forced to leave the paving. The passage of armies made these wider, and tore them up badly in wet weather. The mass of men and horses on the move

ABOVE The earth strip along the roadside has been laid, using Celluclay pre-coloured with sandy acrylic paint, and the face of the bank has been treated in the same way.

TOP The tree stumps, made from balsa dowel with roots from Duro, and coated with Flexibark and Duro.

ABOVE The stumps in place on the top of the bank. The vegetation is made up from rubberised horsehair and Woodland Scenic scatter; and note the rabbit holes. For a finishing touch, you could always add a small dump of lead bird-shot below these.

ABOVE RIGHT An overhead view showing the hollow tree stump; note the fungus on the nearest stump.

probably spent most of their marches slogging along these muddy side-lanes, leaving the paved road for the heavy wagons and artillery trains.

I recreated this earth strip with an area of Celluclay, though to a fairly narrow measure. In reality they could easily be as wide again as the pavement on both sides, but I simply did not have the room, so I used my 'bank' to provide a visual excuse. The Celluclay was then suitably indented with wheel marks and foot- and hoofprints. When this was all done I blended the soil strip into the paved edge of the roadway, and washed it over with my soil colour, picking out the ruts with a lighter shade.

Next I made up some tree stumps from balsa dowel, to add to the bank; I varied them a bit by having two of them hollowed out. I also coated two with Flexibark for a rough-textured finish, to contrast with the smooth finish obtained by using Duro to coat the other two. The

above-ground roots were also shaped from Duro, smoothed onto the stumps and then blended into the surface of the bank. After scribing in bark patterns I painted the stumps with an undercoat of grey-green and highlighted the ribbing of the bark with a paler shade of the same colour. The fungus growth on one stump was also made from Duro and coloured with acrylic orange. Once dry, I added some ivy leaves to the largest stump, made from catkin seeds. I painted the first layer of leaves in a glossy dark green shade and then the top layer in a lighter shade of green, which adds depth to the appearance of leaf cover.

Once the stumps were in place I sprayed the bank, a section at a time, with Scenic Cement and scattered on a layer of fairly coarse ground cover. On top of this I added a layer of rubberised horsehair to represent coarse undergrowth, stuck on with PVA. This was then sprinkled with more flock and left to dry. I added a bit of detail to the sandy face of the bank by digging a couple of rabbit holes; using some fine wire, I made some roots emerging from the soil, colouring these an earthy brown.

To add some interest to the road itself I rummaged in the spares boxes until I came up with a Historex kit, and built a Napoleonic wheelbarrow. I painted it military green, and left it standing with a pile of sets waiting to be used to repair the road bed.

Incidentally, the book by Coppens and Courcelle taught me another pleasing point of detail: that the road from Charleroi had carried the coal wagons from the mines to Brussels for generations. One Captain Duthilt wrote that it was covered with greasy black coal dust, and in rainy weather all troops and horses using it quickly became filthy. In a mild gesture towards this fact I finished the vignette by applying a thin wash of artist's black oil paint across the whole roadway and working in a few smudges of black pastel chalk here and there - an effect which is certainly a lot cleaner than the real thing would have been on 17/18 June 1815.

LEFT Detail of the Historex wheel barrow, with a load of granite sets, standing by the roadside.

LEFT The finished scene, with the roadway suitably grubby with coal dust. Ivy leaves, made from silver birch catkin seeds, grow up the large stump, and tree roots grow out from the face of the bank. Dumps of paving stones were sometimes left at intervals beside main roads for making repairs. Heavy traffic, winter freezing and splitting and spring thaws will tear holes in even modern surfaces.

CHAPTER 11
MODERN SURFACES

This chapter title is perhaps a slight misnomer, since it groups one main vignette using cobbles (which have been used for many hundreds of years) in a 20th century setting, with brief descriptions of more modern poured surfaces. Let us not get hung up on semantics, however.

POURED SURFACES:

CONCRETE HARDSTAND

This piece of groundwork is a very simple base for an aircraft model. I marked off the area for the semi-circle of hardstand and the grass edging of the airfield. I next marked out a cross to represent the seams where the concrete slabs meet, and lightly scribed this into the surface of the baseboard. I used black artist's oil paint, squeezed neat from the tube so that it was very thick, and applied it along the scribe lines as the tar seams.

RIGHT Concrete hardstand - the board marked out with shallow grooves for the seams between the concrete sections.

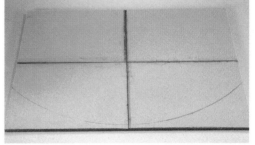

RIGHT Adding the first layer of scatter. The old foil baking tray helps keep all the spillage under control, so you can collect it for later use. The shape of the area that is to be covered in scatter is determined by the area you cover with PVA adhesive to start with.

RIGHT The board covered with concrete-coloured paint. The seams are still just visible.

I then spread PVA over the area to be grassed, and scattered a layer of tan ground cover, over which I added another layer of finer scatter in green, to create the appearance of fairly scruffy-looking grass and weeds. While I was spreading the scatter I put the baseboard in a foil cooking tray; this kept all the flock that spilled over the edges under control and it was easy to pour the excess back into a bag for later use.

Once the grass was set, I painted the hardstand area with a concrete-coloured matt paint mix. When this was dry I spread a fine layer of concrete-coloured pastel chalk powder all over the hardstand, working it into the board with my fingertips. I mixed up a very thin wash of black acrylic and water in a saucer, and let drops of this wash drip from the end of my brush into the cement powder, keeping the brush away from the surface to prevent any obvious brush marks. The thin wash spread naturally into the dry powder, looking like old oil stains on the concrete. If you wish you can add a slightly darker centre to these stains for a bit of colour variety. I also touched in the 'tar' seams to bring them out again from the cement. To finish off I cut a simple stencil from some thin acrylic sheet and sprayed in the white lines at the edge of the hardstand.

ASPHALT & TAR MACADAM

There is very little to be said about these two modern road surfaces. To create an asphalt road all you need do is get some fine Wet & Dry paper, and stick it down to the baseboard with PVA glue with the grey, textured side uppermost. Add some washes and darker stains, and any road markings you may want - and the job is done.

Tar macadam has a different appearance to asphalt. It has an almost blue tone in the colour, and also a slightly shinier finish. To create this effect on the vignette I sprayed the board with Scenic Cement and then spread a layer of the tar macadam medium made by Javis Scenics. I used a flour shaker to spread this in an even coat and then, before it had dried, I rolled it as flat as I could with a small wooden hand roller. I repeated this about four times until I had a solid layer of 'macadam' on the board, and then sealed the last coat with Scenic Cement. When this had dried I sprayed on the white lines.

LEFT The finished hardstand. The tar seams have been picked out with undiluted artist's black oil paint, and oil stains added by flicking the tip of the brush, loaded with a very wet mix of black acrylic paint, over the pastel dust so that it automatically spreads into a stain. The white lines were made using a simple stencil and matt white paint.

LEFT Asphalt at the top, and below the kerbing tar macadam. The difference is just about visible; the tar macadam has slightly more texture than the asphalt, and has a slightly blue-black sheen.

RIGHT The polystyrene block has been hollowed out for the crater and coated with the first, sealing layer of Celluclay. The plaster pavement section is glued to the back, with some paving slabs cut free and tilted at an angle. This photo also shows why I didn't persevere with using split peas for the cobblestones.

A SHELL CRATER

This model represents a small section of cobbled street that has been shelled. Many streets in Europe during World War II were still cobbled like this, and it isn't too difficult to recreate this type of road surface using pellets of Granitex for the cobbles.

As I wanted to have a fairly deep crater I used a block of expanded polystyrene for the base rather than MDF. First I marked out the areas of the crater and of the pavement, and then excavated the hole with a scalpel. This done, I used a plaster casting of a section of resin pavement that I had in my stock box. I cut some of the paving stones away from the casting so that I could set them at an angle in the rubble of the explosion. Next came a layer of earth-coloured Celluclay, which I spread

RIGHT & BELOW Farewell, split peas... The pavement has received its first layer of colour, and the base of the shattered brick wall has been set in place. I've set the various bits of rusted iron pipes in the crater walls and muddied them up.

LEFT A layer of brick-coloured Celluclay has been spread at the base of the wall. The idea here is two fold: first-ly, it forms an adhesive to hold the rest of the individual loose bricks, and secondly, any gaps between the bricks will blend with the rest of the rubble. A second application of Celluclay has been applied all over the inside of the crater in as lumpy and rough a layer as possible.

BELOW The first lot of cobbles go down; these are 3mm moulded balls of Granitex and, in my opinion, look much better than the split peas.

over the roadbed and to line the crater. This first layer in the crater was merely to seal the polystyrene and to make a basis for a second, much rougher coat. I added this second layer to give the impression of ruptured, torn-up lumps and clods of earth; the first coat would have been far too smooth for this effect.

To make a backdrop for the scene I built up the remains of a brick wall, using bricks which I cast from plaster in a silicone mould. To dress up the crater I decided to include some twisted iron pipes and a ruptured water main. The pipes are simply bent lengths of wire, painted a suitable rusty colour and pushed into the sides of the crater.

The water main is made from a plastic drinking straw. It is a reasonable size in diameter and, when cut open, the walls are a good scale thickness. I cut three short lengths of straw, two for the longer section of broken pipe and one for the stump sticking out of the opposite wall. I cut two discs of cardboard for the flanges and then punched out eight 'bolt heads' from a sheet of plasticard. After sticking a flange onto each half of the longer pipe section, I stuck these two together and glued four bolt heads to each face of the flange, front and back.

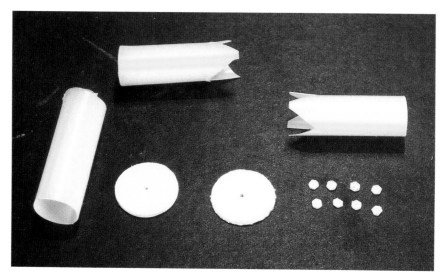

RIGHT The component parts of the shattered water main: three short lengths of plastic drinking straw, two cardboard discs for the flanges, and eight bolt heads punched from plasticard with a Historex hexagonal Punch & Die set.

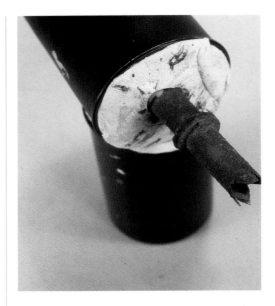

RIGHT One half of the finished water main.

RIGHT Making the spout of water from the shattered main - uneven lengths of optic fibres are glued together to make the armature.

RIGHT The armature covered with Artist's Gloss Medium and tinted with Vitrail olive green glass paint.

When all were dry I painted the pipes with a rusting medium called Rustall. At the moment I believe this is only available from the States - my supply comes from the Micro Mark company. You just paint this over the pipe and leave it to dry. If the result is not rusty enough for you, just lay on another coat, and so on until you're happy with the amount of 'corrosion'. When the coats were dry I then went over the pipe with two different shades of another rust product which also came from America. Produced by a company called Pre-size Models, they were marketed under the name FX Weathering Compounds. They were a excellent product since, when dry, they not only gave you new, medium and heavy rust colours, but they also had a rough, corroded texture. (I have also mentioned in earlier chapters their FX Mud.) Sadly, I believe the 'FX' range is no longer available, and I'm hoarding my last few pots like a miser. If you come across this anywhere, grab it, and if any of my readers in the States know where I could still get some - please get in touch!

While on the subject of rust, a new product marketed by the British company Accurate Armour under the name Instant Rust also recreates the rough, scabby texture of rusty metal. This is a two-part medium which requires the first coat to be left for about 12 hours before adding the next, but the result is worth the wait.

Anyway, back to the crater. To create the impression of water pouring from the broken pipe I took some short lengths of an old bit of fibre optic that was lying around (but any transparent strip of plastic material will do), and stuck them together with PVA. The idea was to make a transparent armature on which I could build up the stream of water. This I did by adding uneven blobs of Artist's Gloss Medium, which is a white, creamy-textured material, available in small pots from almost any art shop. When it dries it is almost transparent. When I had built up enough I coloured it with a very thin application of an olive green paint which is used for decorating glassware. The particular brand I used here is called Vitrail, but there are many others available in art shops.

Once the 'water spout' had dried I gave it several coats of gloss varnish, and set it aside while I mixed the resin for the water in the crater. Before pouring the water into the hole I coloured the lower part of the crater walls with a greyish shade of soil colour; the soil at a depth is usually darker and damper than that nearer the surface. Once again I used a 50/50

LEFT The water, made with 50/50 resin very lightly dyed with Vitrail olive green glass paint. Both layers have been poured; I added the stream of water from the ruptured main before pouring in the second, so as to be sure that the end would be below the water level. You can also see some of the bricks under the water, added along with various bits of rusty iron before I poured the second layer.

BELOW Detail of the brick rubble and the abandonded jerry can. I cast the bricks in a silicone mould from pre-coloured plaster.

mix of resin and hardener and, at the same time, added in a drop of the olive green glass paint. (I emphasize the word 'drop'; a little of this paint goes a long way, and it is easy to make too dense a colour). I poured my first layer of resin into the crater and left it to set.

While waiting, I stuck the spout of water into the end of the water main, using PVA, and positioned it over the surface. I added debris in the water, and a length of rusty girder. When the resin had set I poured a second layer in, and made sure it came high enough up the crater so that the end of the stream of water from the pipe was just covered.

Once the second layer of resin had set I began making the ripples and foam caused by the stream of water. First I built up the ripples by adding semi-circles of gloss medium spreading out from under the end of the pipe and, once these had set, I gently stippled matt white paint in circles until I had my foam effect. The last touch was to add some mud to the various exposed lengths of pipework. Now it was time to lay my cobbled road surface.

I have included a shot of my first efforts at laying cobbles to illustrate why you shouldn't always believe everything you read in modelling magazines! I had read on many occasions that the best and quickest way to make a cobbled road was to use dried split peas. Raiding the larder, I started to lay the street, but it very quickly became obvious that the average split pea was too large to represent

a cobblestone in 1/35th or 1/32nd scale. I realize that not all cobbles are the same size, but take a look at a street near you or find a photo, and you'll see what I mean. Unless you have a supply of very small split peas, forget it.

I decided to make the stones from Granitex. I rolled out a lump into a ribbon and cut it up into small pieces, which I then rolled into balls of about 3mm–4mm diameter. When I judged that I had enough to cover one end of the street, I put these in the oven on a foil baking tray and left them for about ten minutes at 135 degrees C. When they were done I spread a thin layer of Celluclay on the road and pressed the cobbles into it, one at a time, leaving a small gap between each one. When they were all in place I made up some more Celluclay and grouted them in. While they set I repeated the process for the rest of the model, and then left it overnight.

The next day I gently rubbed over the surface of the cobbles with a fine Wet & Dry paper, just to create the impression of wear, and then applied a wash of Raw Umber over the whole street. This tended to form a darker shade on the Celluclay grouting, thus creating a natural contrast with the lighter stones. I then added some more spoil over the cobbles nearest the crater, and dry-brushed all around the lip. Finally I added some more rubble and odd cobble stones into the soil; an old jerrycan was dumped in the brick rubble together with a couple of rusty girders, and my urban shell crater was finished.

RIGHT The Granitex from which I made the cobbles, lying on the silicone mould which I used to cast the individual plaster bricks (and, incidentally, the Granitex granite sets for the model of the Napoleonic road in Chapter 10).

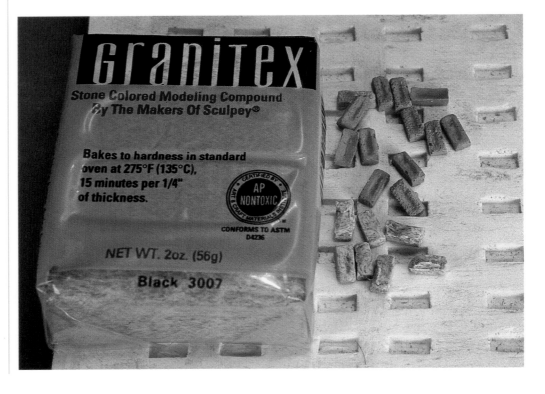

LEFT The second layer of resin has set and I have started to work up the froth around the end of the stream of water. I used Artist's Gloss Medium applied in a stippled fashion, working round in semi-circles. The length of RSJ was also put in at this point. This photo dramatically captures the meniscus effect - in fact it looks worse here than it does to the naked eye. In such a confined space neither of the tricks described in Chapter 8 could be applied.

LEFT More circles of Gloss Medium are added and a touch of off-white paint is used to create the foam. To give the impression of the water foaming under the surface and to create the illusion of depth, I've added a thin wash of the olive green glass paint over the white foam at the outer edge of the disturbed water.

LEFT Overall shot of the finished crater, with the final pieces of debris in position. Note that after grouting with Celluclay only the top surfaces of the Granitex pellets show 'above ground', and that the cobbles have been slightly smoothed over to create a worn appearance.

CHAPTER 12
SNOW & ICE

RIGHT The basis of the frozen river vignette. A strip of clear plastic has had candle wax 'air bubbles' added to the underside and Glass Etch frosting has been sprayed on the top. Now it is glued down to the baseboard; the black strip painted along the middle of the base is almost hidden, but still suggests the darkness of deep water underneath the ice.

RIGHT The basic areas of the river banks built up with Celluclay, over the edges of the strip of 'ice'.

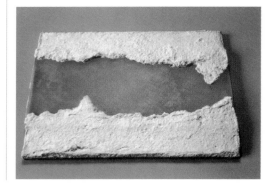

BELOW Pads of newspaper secured to the Celluclay with masking tape form the uneven humps of the river bank.

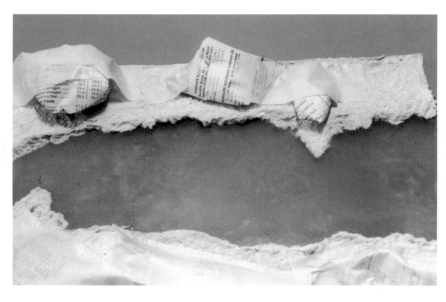

Snow and ice are fairly easy to recreate in a model, and a number of materials and techniques are described under Snow Effects in Chapter 1, so I won't repeat myself here at any length.

For a scene covered with really heavy snow and deep drifts the best medium is a thick mixture of plaster of Paris. Stir this smoothly together until you get the right consistency; plaster is cheap, and you can easily practice by pouring it over bits of polystyrene scrap and folded card until it moves and stops just as you want. Pour it from above, adding it generously to the groundwork, over logs, rocks, etc.. Unless you are modelling a completely snow-covered scene, remember to leave a gap between the lower edge of the snow on top of these features and the ground, so that you can still see the side surfaces. When adding it to roofs, pour from the ridge and let it run right down to the eaves and form a heavy bulge hanging over the edge.

Check your reference photos; you will want to reproduce the ways in which snow collects along the upper surfaces of branches, walls and fences, and the lumps it forms in the forks of trees. A really heavy fall will bend slender trees over and drag the branches of older trees down. Telephone cables will sag under the weight; recreating these effects will add realism to your winter scene.

If you just want to add a dusting of snow to the scene, use poly-beads scattered from your flour shaker and held in place with an indirect misting of hairspray. You can gently blow it about in swirls on the groundwork to simulate the effect of the wind on powdery snow. For a frosty finish to groundwork, buildings or vehicles, airbrush a very thin mixture of acrylic white over the scene, making sure that the colours underneath can still show through. Remember that a modest addition of finely-ground Alum BP will give your snow 'sparkle'. Practice using all these mediums, separately and in combination, until you are confident.

ICICLES

I have made icicles hanging from the eaves of a model house the lazy way, by using

FAR LEFT A layer of plaster bandage is laid over the newspaper; and the old tree trunk is added to the bank. I am about to drill a small hole at an angle into the plastic 'ice' to fix a washed-up 'branch' (made from a small twig) to one bank.

ABOVE RIGHT The heavy snow covering has been added with poured plaster, together with the winter skeleton of a tree. On the right a branch has been washed up onto a spur of the river bank, and I have added animal tracks coming down to the water's edge. Powder snow dusts the ice near the banks.

LEFT & BELOW Two angles on the frozen river, photographed against a winter afternoon sky.

ready-made plastic ones from an old Faller Winter Scene kit I picked up years ago. You just glue them in place along the eaves and drip on layers of gloss varnish until you have the length you want. I realize that this kit is probably not around any more, so here are couple of ways of making your own icicles.

The first way is to support a strip of wood or plasticard by its ends across a gap between two rests, in an edge-up position. Put small blobs of PVA glue at intervals along the bottom edge. When they are set, get some 'stringy' glue like polystyrene cement and squeeze a drop onto each blob of PVA. Draw it downward into a long drip and leave it to dry. Repeat this process until you are satisfied with the general size and shape of your icicle. When it is dry, run drops of gloss varnish down the icicle and let this dry too. Remember that a strip of icicles are not all the same length. Keep adding varnish until you are happy with the result, and leave your strip of icicles to set overnight. In the morning, use a sharp scalpel to gently cut the blobs of PVA free in one strip along the base of your row of icicles, and glue it to your roof, tree or whatever.

TOP The piece of clear plastic for the icy pond cut roughly to shape, and with the melted candle wax 'air bubbles' visible on the underside.

CENTRE The layout for the groundwork: Celluclay covers the baseboard and the edges of the black cardboard 'water'. The fallen tree trunk is a piece of natural driftwood.

BOTTOM The plaster has been poured over the ground and the tree and, before it set, I planted clumps of dead grass at various places. The snow doesn't have to be absolutely featureless - it forms mounds of various sizes and shapes over buried vegetation - but all the surfaces should look rounded and untouched. If you mess around with it you lose the benefit of a poured finish.

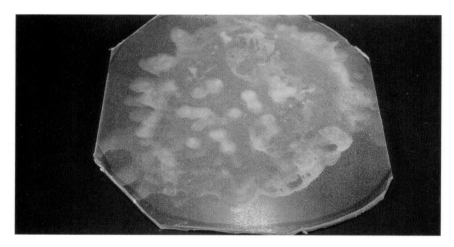

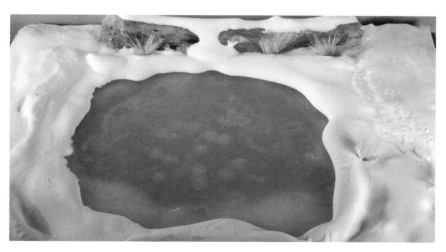

The second method is to get hold of some scraps of optic fibre as the basis of the icicle. Set them up on the edge of a piece of wood, as described above; then add layers of Artist's Gloss Medium, building it up fairly thickly at the top and drawing it to a taper, allowing it to dry between each layer. When you have the shape you want, leave it overnight; then add coats of gloss varnish to achieve a nice cold sparkle.

A FROZEN RIVER & AN ICY POND

Creating the effect of frozen water is quite easy. Start with a piece of clear plastic or polycarbonate. Take a candle stub and melt drops of wax onto the surface of the plastic in an irregular pattern. Next, you need an iron; cover the wax blobs with greaseproof paper, then smooth the blobs down by passing the iron fairly briefly across the paper. The paper will stop the wax adhering to the sole plate of the iron (and probably save you from a fate worse than death at the hands of the owner of the iron).

Next, take your baseboard and paint a strip of black up the centre, narrower than the strip of plastic. Apply PVA glue to the edges of the under (waxy) side of the plastic, and stick it down to the board so that the glued strips are either side of the black-painted portion. Once this is set you need an aerosol of Humbrol Glass Etch spray. This is a product intended for use on decorative glasswork; when sprayed on it gives the same effect as glass that has been frosted by etching with sand. The effect you will achieve is that of an icy surface, partly opaque, but with the dark water of the river partially visible through the ice, with the blobs of candle wax giving the appearance of air pockets trapped under the ice.

The riverbanks are built up in the usual way with Celluclay, carried over the edges of the 'frozen' plastic strip and making irregular shapes where the banks and water meet. To build up the lumpy surface of the banks for this vignette I next added wads of newspaper rolled into bun shapes and taped down with masking tape. (This is often a quick and easy method of shaping your groundwork if you don't have lumps of polystyrene available.) I covered the newspaper lumps and the rest of the riverbanks with plaster bandage, adding at this point anything that I wanted to have poking up through the snow - in this case an old tree trunk.

To make the snow, I made up a thick mix of modelling plaster to the point where it would

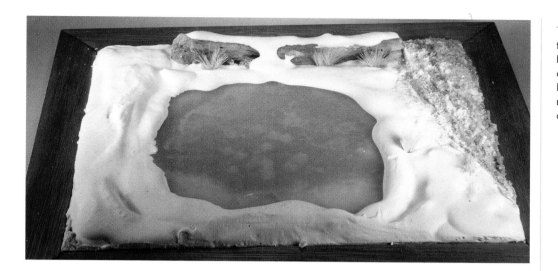

TOP & CENTRE The area of frozen, slightly muddy slush has been added at the top right corner of the vignette. I used Hudson & Allen Studio 'Slush', mixed with water and a touch of earthy acrylic paint.

LEFT The final touch is fine, powdery snow drifted over the ice. This is made with fine poly-beads from 4D Models.

BELOW The final touch - a shivering redcoat pauses by the pond, perhaps on his way to Corunna in January 1809? This figure was kindly painted for me by Charles Davis.

only just pour, and then slopped it in a controlled way over the riverbanks, fallen tree, rocks, etc. and left it to set. As I was using a pretty thick mixture this took quite a while. The idea is to achieve a smooth, rounded finish like untouched virgin snow – you should have the patience to leave the plaster to set without pushing it around with your spatula.

When the snow had set, I drilled a small hole in the ice and set in a tree branch snagged on the river's edge; then I put in a bare tree on the bank. The branches of the tree were also treated to a small amount of the thick plaster, and I scattered a drifting of fine poly-beads along each bank.

The model of the **icy pond** was made in much the same way as that of the frozen river. There are obviously no large humps made from newspaper under the snow, but the ice and the thick snow were made in exactly the same way; in this case I used a piece of black card rather than a painted area to provide the darkness under my 'ice'. The log is a small piece of driftwood, and the dead grasses are from a pack of Woodland Scenics Field Grass. The only difference here is that I have added an area of churned-up, frozen slush.

This can be done by mixing baking powder with PVA to create a 'lumpy' look; but personally, while I think this is a good method for showing packed snow in tank or truck suspensions or under mudguards, I feel it lacks the true sparkle of semi-icy slush. There are a couple of ways to achieve this effect. The first is to make up a mixture of PVA glue and Alum BP. Apart from mixing it in with the plaster or poly-beads which you have used to make your snow to add reflective points, you can just use it on its own to get a really frozen, slushy look.

The second way, which is what I did here, is to buy one of Hudson & Allen's packets of 'Slush'. Just mix this with water until you get the desired consistency, then spread it onto your groundwork and leave to dry. If you want an area of dirty slush, just mix in some colouring with the water. Slush is one of a number of products produced by Hudson & Allen for us 'groundhogs'; they also market Mud, Snow and other useful ground effects, and they are all worth the money.

LEFT An experiment in photography: to get an even colder look I used a blue filter over the lens when taking this one.

LEFT Tracks in snow, which tends to show up the detail of tyre treads well. While your plaster is still damp, run a truck tyre through it until you have a good imprint. It helps to rinse the tyre after each pass, otherwise it clogs up.

Let the plaster dry; then pick out the 'lowlights' - the depressions of the pattern - with an earthy colour, leaving the ridges white. This creates both visual depth, and the effect of mud underneath being churned up by the tyres. Build up a ridge of dirty snow either side of each tyre track where it has been forced aside by the passage of the wheel.

ABOVE 'The Derelict': this is a diorama which I built sometime ago, depicting a burnt-out Stuart in the Ardennes. The tree was my first attempt at following Barry Bowen's method. The rusting was applied after I had built and painted the model. I'm a great believer in applying weathering over a completely finished painting and marking scheme. In real life, rust or scorching won't hide all the original markings. By adding all the stars and serial numbers before starting on the rust you get a very realistic finish, with faint markings showing through the weathering.

RIGHT & CENTRE Further angles on 'The Derelict'. In this case the impression was obviously that the tank had burned before the most recent snow fall. A vehicle which has burned in snow-covered terrain will melt an area all around it, which will then re-freeze, filling any tracks or other depressions with smooth new ice, in which any debris of the explosion will be frozen.

RIGHT The frozen slush around 'The Derelict' is from Hudson & Allen Studio, and the frozen puddle just visible at bottom right is a drop of candle wax, levelled out by holding a hot iron above it.

ABOVE Part of an Iron Age village (c800-0 BC) in the depths of winter, modelled in 1/62nd scale for the Zug museum. The snow in this scene is once again thick plaster; the houses are the usual cardboard shells covered with plaster castings and held together with PVA glue; the gatehouse is made from bass wood with cast plaster panels of wattle and daub.

LEFT 'Fallschirmjäger, Leningrad Front, 1942'. The bracken is etched brass and the log is a piece of driftwood; note the 'cake icing' effect of the 'broken-off' snow along the top of the log. The para's footprints have trodden some bracken down into the area of slushy snow - I made the footprints using the feet from the kit. The icicle is a piece of clear plastic built up with gloss varnish.

ABOVE Another of the 1/62nd scale Zug dioramas was to depict a Paleolithic hunting camp of c13000-5000 BC. The lake water is made with Nimix Artificial Water gel; I did not add any colouring since at this period in history the water would be unpolluted. The appearance of depth can be obtained by painting the lakebed a darker shade the further away you get from the shore. The tents are made from thin copper sheet, with poles made from tiny twigs emerging from the apex; for their light coating of powder snow they received a mist of hairspray before I scattered them with poly-beads. The base is plaster, scattered with ground cover. The stones weighting down the skirts of the tents and scattered on the lakebed are Woodland Scenics Talus.

ABOVE Details from the Paleolithic hunting camp. The birches are simply painted twigs; the dwarf junipers are railway modelling 'ready-made' fir trees cut down. All the light snow on the vegetation is made with flicks of white paint and scattered poly-beads.

APPENDIX

The following list of sources for products are those which I have used, living in the south of England; in the case of retail outlets readers should obviously check with manufacturers in case a more local stockist is available.

BOOKS

Woodland Scenics, PO Box 98, Linn Creek, MO 65052, USA 'The Scenery Manual' - an excellent 'how to' book on the Woodland Scenics range. A video is also available.

Barry Bowen 'Trees' - this very useful duplicated booklet, which considerably extends the information quoted by permission in Chapter 4 of the present book, is available from the author at £4.99. Telephone (0)1474-352860 (UK) to order a copy by post.

Historex Agents, Wellington House, 157 Snargate Street, Dover, Kent CT17 9BZ, UK. Tel (0)1304-206720; fax (0)1304-204528. 'How to Build Dioramas' and 'Modelling Tanks & Military Vehicles' by Shep Paine, published by Kalmbach in the USA.

Model World, Newnham Court Centre, Bearsted Road, Maidstone, Kent ME14 5LH, UK. Tel (0)1622-735586, fax (0)1622-735581. Woodland Scenics 'The Scenery Manual', and the Woodland Scenics video.

Tondeur Diffusion, 9 Av. Fr.Van Kalken, 1070 Bruxelles, Belgium Tel 0032-2-555-0218, fax 0032-2-555-0219. Distributors of 'Waterloo 1815: Les Carnets de la Campagne' by B.Coppens & P.Courcelle; Nos.1 to 4 available at the time of writing - see comment under 'A Napoleonic Road' in Chapter 10.

MATERIALS & TOOLS (USA)

Hudson & Allen Studio, PO Box 82341, Rochester, MI 48307 Various scenic materials, including packets of 'Snow', 'Slush' and 'Mud'.

Micro-Mark, 340 Snyder Avenue, Berkley Heights, NJ 07922-1595 Supplier of a wide range of excellent tools for the modeller, as well as a number of scenic materials and weathering agents.

A.West, PO Box 1144, Woodstock, GA 30188 'Weather-It', an instant weathering chemical which penetrates wood and produces the time-worn 'silvery' effect on the newest surface.

Woodland Scenics (address as above) Ground covers, static grass, snow, Rock Molds, earth & rock colouring kits, Scenic Cement, Field Grass, E-Z-Water, tree kits, poly-fibre, Hydrocal lightweight plaster, Talus, Hob-e-Tac glue, and many other materials for building dioramas.

MATERIALS & TOOLS (UK)

4D Model Shop, 151 City Road, London EC1V 1JH Tel (0)20-7253-1996, fax (0)20-7253-1998. Foam board, Flexibark, rubberised horsehair; a wide range of scenic materials including tree kits, ground cover, rocks, etc. sold under the name 'Green Scene'; and a useful range of adhesives. A catalogue is available covering a range of products and tools that will be of interest to all modellers - also available in CD format.

Gaugemaster Controls plc, Gaugemaster House, Ford Road, Arundel, W.Sussex BN18 0BN Grass and gravel matting, plus a range of other scenic materials.

Historex Agents (address as above). Andrea range of acrylic water colours; Nimix Artificial Water; Historex punch & die set.

Hythe (Kent) Model Shop, 153A High Street, Hythe, Kent CT21 5JL Tel (0)1303-267236. Bass wood, balsa wood; some of the Woodland Scenics range; Javis Countryside Scenics ground covers, including 'Rough Meadow' and 'Tar Macadam'. Also stocks the Anita Décor range of scenic materials, and the new Hydro-Fibre.

Model World (address as above) Stockists of the Woodland Scenics and Javis Countryside Scenics ranges of ground covers.

Newnham Court Crafts, Newnham Court Centre, Bearsted Road, Maidstone, Kent ME14 5LH Tel/Fax (0) 1622-630886 Refillable plastic aerosols, sold under name Arty's.

Scale Link Ltd, Iwerne Minster, Dorset DT11 8Q Tel/fax (0)1747-811817/812250. Wide range of etched brass foliage. Catalogue available.

Alex Tiranti Ltd, 78 High Street, Theale, Reading, Berks RG7 5AR Tel (0) 118-930-2775 All necessary equipment, supplies and instructions for a range of home casting techniques, plus other modelling materials and tools. Catalogue available.

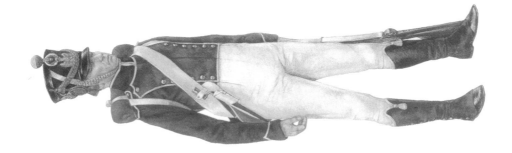

OSPREY PUBLISHING

FIND OUT MORE ABOUT OSPREY

❑ Please send me a FREE trial issue
   of Osprey Military Journal

❑ Please send me the latest listing of Osprey's publications

❑ I would like to subscribe to Osprey's e-mail newsletter

Title/rank _____

Name _____

Address _____

_____

Postcode/zip _____ state/country _____

e-mail _____

Which book did this card come from?

_____

❑ I am interested in military history

My preferred period of military history is _____

❑ I am interested in military aviation

My preferred period of military aviation is _____

I am interested in (please tick all that apply)

❑ general history   ❑ militaria   ❑ model making
❑ wargaming   ❑ re-enactment

Please send to:

USA & Canada: Osprey Direct USA, c/o Motorbooks
International, P.O. Box 1, 729 Prospect Avenue, Osceola,
WI 54020

UK, Europe and rest of world:
Osprey Direct UK, P.O. Box 140, Wellingborough, Northants,
NN8 2FA, United Kingdom

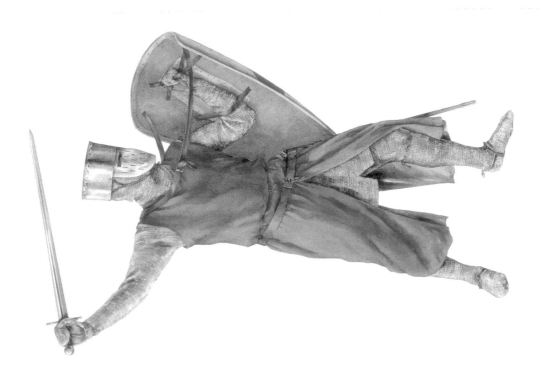

O OSPREY
PUBLISHING

www.ospreypublishing.com

call our telephone hotline
for a free information pack

USA & Canada: 1-800-458-0454
UK, Europe and rest of world call:
+44 (0) 1933 443 863

Young Guardsman
Figure taken from *Warrior 22:
Imperial Guardsman 1799–1815*
Published by Osprey
Illustrated by Christa Hook

Knight, c.1190
Figure taken from *Warrior 1: Norman Knight 950 – 1204AD*
Published by Osprey
Illustrated by Christa Hook

POSTCARD